Thunder Bay
Travel Guide 2024
Explore the Stunning Natural Beauty, Outdoor Activities, and Off-the-Beaten-Path in Canada's Untamed North

Lovelyn Hill

Dedication

I dedicate this guidebook to those captivated by Thunder Bay. May it be your trusted companion through your remarkable journey to Thunder Bay.

Table of Contents

Part 1

Planning Your Thunder Bay Adventure

Introduction

Welcome to the "Thunder Bay Travel Guide 2024," your passport to an extraordinary adventure in the heart of Canada's untamed north. In the pages that follow, you will embark on a journey that goes beyond the ordinary, inviting you to explore the stunning natural beauty, engage in thrilling outdoor activities, and uncover the hidden gems that make Thunder Bay a distinctive and captivating destination.

Discover Thunder Bay's Natural Splendor

As you dive into this guide, the breathtaking landscapes of Thunder Bay unfold before you. From the majestic presence of Lake Superior to the rugged beauty of Sleeping Giant Provincial Park, the untamed north invites you to witness nature at its most awe-inspiring. The guide not only introduces you to these iconic landmarks but also reveals lesser-known treasures, ensuring that every moment of your adventure is filled with wonder.

Immerse Yourself in Outdoor Adventures

Feel the adrenaline surge as you navigate the diverse outdoor activities Thunder Bay has to offer. Whether you're a seasoned adventurer or a first-time explorer, this guide equips you with the knowledge to embark on hiking trails that range from easy strolls to challenging treks. Dive into the crystal-clear waters of Lake Superior for kayaking and paddleboarding, or embrace the thrill of fishing and hunting in the vast wilderness. In the winter, transform Thunder Bay into your personal wonderland with skiing, snowshoeing, and dog sledding experiences that will leave you enchanted.

Off-the-Beaten-Path Gems Await

Beyond the well-trodden trails, Thunder Bay conceals hidden gems that add a touch of magic to your journey. Unearth sparkling treasures at the Blue Point Amethyst Mine, where you can dig for your amethyst and carry home a piece of Thunder Bay's geological wonders. Witness the awe-inspiring Kakabeka Falls, a natural wonder that captivates with its cascading beauty. Explore the Sleeping Giant Provincial Park and stand in awe of the iconic formation that defines Thunder Bay's skyline. The Terry Fox Monument pays tribute to a Canadian hero, adding a touch of inspiration to your exploration.

Tailor Your Adventure with Itineraries

To ensure your journey suits your preferences, the guide presents curated itineraries designed for various travel styles. Whether you seek an action-packed adventure over three days, a family-friendly weekend filled with joyous activities, a romantic escapade for two, or a solo exploration that celebrates independence, Thunder Bay welcomes you with open arms.

Unveil Thunder Bay's Rich History and Culture

Delve into the historical riches of Thunder Bay, where Indigenous heritage and traditions intertwine with the legacy of the fur trade era. Fort William Historical Park stands as a testament to the region's past, offering a glimpse into the challenges and triumphs of a bygone era. Immerse yourself in Thunder Bay's vibrant arts and culture scene through galleries, museums, and local festivals. Indulge in the flavors of the region with culinary delights that reflect the diversity and richness of Thunder Bay's cultural tapestry.

In the pages of the "Thunder Bay Travel Guide 2024," you are not just a traveler; you are an adventurer, ready to embrace the wonders that await in Canada's untamed north. Let the guide be your compass, guiding you through an unforgettable exploration of Thunder Bay's stunning natural beauty, thrilling outdoor activities, and off-the-beaten-path treasures. Your adventure begins now.

Why Thunder Bay?

Thunder Bay, with its majestic landscapes and unspoiled beauty, stands as a testament to nature's grandeur. As you venture into this captivating destination, you'll find yourself surrounded by the breathtaking scenery that defines Canada's untamed north. Lake Superior, the world's largest freshwater lake, embraces the city, offering expansive views and an immediate connection to the pure and untouched wilderness.

In Thunder Bay, the allure of nature is not a distant spectacle; it's an immersive experience. As you explore the rugged terrains of Sleeping Giant Provincial Park, you'll be captivated by the iconic Sleeping Giant formation, a geological wonder that adds a dramatic touch to the city's skyline. Feel the cool breeze on your face as you hike through the lush forests and discover hidden gems, from serene lakes nestled between ancient trees to panoramic vistas that showcase the untamed beauty of Thunder Bay.

Thrill Seekers, Rejoice

For the adventurous soul within you, Thunder Bay is a playground of excitement and outdoor activities. Lace up your hiking boots and embark on a journey through a network of trails that cater to every level of hiker. From strolls to challenging treks, Thunder

Bay's diverse landscapes provide a canvas for your outdoor escapades.

Feel the exhilaration as you paddle across the pristine waters of Lake Superior. Kayaking and paddleboarding offer a unique perspective of the city's coastline, allowing you to navigate crystal-clear waters while being surrounded by the untouched beauty of the north. Fishing enthusiasts will find paradise in Thunder Bay, where the lakes and rivers teem with a variety of fish species, creating an angler's haven.

As winter blankets Thunder Bay in snow, the adventure continues. Strap on your skis or snowshoes and glide through snow-covered landscapes. The city transforms into a winter wonderland, inviting you to embrace the cold with open arms. Engage in the thrill of dog sledding, an experience that combines the beauty of the landscape with the power and grace of sled dogs, creating memories that will last a lifetime.

Off-the-Beaten-Path Delights

Beyond the well-trodden paths, Thunder Bay unveils its hidden treasures, waiting to be discovered by intrepid travelers like yourself. Venture to the Blue Point Amethyst Mine, where you have the unique opportunity to unearth your sparkling amethyst gems. The thrill of digging into the Earth and revealing these geological wonders adds a touch of magic to your journey.

Kakabeka Falls, a breathtaking natural wonder, beckons you to witness the sheer power and beauty of cascading waters. Feel the mist on your face as you stand in awe of this captivating spectacle. Explore the wonders of Sleeping Giant Provincial Park, where every trail reveals a new facet of the iconic Sleeping Giant, inviting you to unravel the mysteries of this geological marvel.

The Terry Fox Monument, a tribute to a Canadian hero, invites you to reflect on courage and resilience. Set against the backdrop of Thunder Bay's natural beauty, this monument adds a poignant touch to your exploration, connecting you to the history and spirit of the region.

Immerse Yourself in Rich History and Vibrant Culture

Thunder Bay's allure extends beyond its natural wonders; it encompasses rich history and culture. Immerse yourself in the Indigenous heritage and traditions that have shaped the identity of this land. Discover the echoes of the fur trade era at Fort William Historical Park, a meticulously reconstructed fur trading post that transports you back in time.

The city's arts and culture scene comes alive in its galleries, museums, and festivals. Dive into the vibrant displays of local artists, unraveling the stories that each piece tells about Thunder Bay's diverse and dynamic culture. Indulge in the flavors of the region, where culinary delights reflect the fusion of traditions, creating a unique gastronomic experience.

A Warm Welcome Awaits

As you traverse the streets of Thunder Bay, you'll be welcomed by the warmth and friendliness of its locals. The city's charm extends beyond its natural wonders and outdoor adventures; it lies in the genuine hospitality of those who call Thunder Bay home.

Savor the culinary delights that Thunder Bay has to offer. From fresh local seafood to Indigenous cuisine and international fare, the city's diverse culinary scene caters to every palate. Whether you're exploring local markets or dining in charming cafes, each bite tells a story of Thunder Bay's rich cultural tapestry.

Practical Considerations

While the allure of Thunder Bay is undeniable, practical considerations ensure that your journey is seamless and enjoyable. Understand the diverse climate of the region, and dress accordingly to make the most of your outdoor adventures. Familiarize yourself with transportation options and local transit to navigate the city with ease.

As you plan your visit, consider the best times to explore Thunder Bay based on your preferred activities. Each season brings its unique charm, from vibrant summer festivals to the serene beauty of winter landscapes. Plan your itinerary to align with your interests and make the most of your time in Canada's untamed north.

Thus, Thunder Bay invites you with open arms, beckoning you to delve into the majesty of its nature, embrace thrilling outdoor adventures, uncover hidden treasures, immerse yourself in rich history and vibrant culture, and experience the warm hospitality of its people. Your journey to Thunder Bay is an exploration of a destination that promises to leave an indelible mark on your heart.

The Perfect Time for Your Thunder Bay

Selecting the ideal time to visit Thunder Bay is pivotal for ensuring you experience the city's diverse offerings to the fullest. Each season brings its charm and activities, allowing you to tailor your visit based on your preferences and desired adventures.

Summer (June - August)

Pros

- Warmest weather, ideal for outdoor activities like hiking, kayaking, and fishing.
- Long daylight hours provide ample time for exploration and adventure.
- Vibrant summer festivals and outdoor events showcase the lively spirit of Thunder Bay.

Cons

- Mosquitoes can be present, especially in wooded areas, so insect repellent is advisable.
- Some hiking trails may be closed due to wet conditions.

Fall (September - November)

Pros

- Pleasant temperatures create perfect conditions for hiking, biking, and scenic drives.
- The fall foliage transforms the landscape into a kaleidoscope of vibrant colors.
- Fewer crowds and lower accommodation prices make it an appealing time for budget-conscious travelers.

Cons

- Water activities become limited as temperatures start to drop.
- Some businesses may close for the season, affecting availability.

Winter (December - February)

Pros

- Thunder Bay transforms into a winter wonderland, offering opportunities for snowshoeing, skiing, and dog sledding.
- Festive winter events and a cozy atmosphere make it an enchanting season to visit.
- The potential for seeing the aurora borealis adds a magical touch to winter nights.

Cons

- Coldest weather and shortest daylight hours limit some outdoor activities.
- Some trails and attractions may be closed due to snow and ice.

Spring (March - May)

Pros

- Warmer temperatures with melting snow make it suitable for early-season hiking and biking.
- Less crowded than summer and fall, providing a quieter experience.
- Spring festivals and events celebrate the return of warmer weather.

Cons

- Some trails may be muddy or waterlogged due to snowmelt.
- Unpredictable weather with occasional snow showers.

Considerations for Your Visit

- Specific Activities: If you have particular activities in mind, research whether they are best enjoyed during a specific season.
- Personal Preferences: Consider your tolerance for different weather conditions and whether you prefer a bustling atmosphere or a quieter experience.
- Budget and Crowds: Determine whether you prioritize lower accommodation prices and fewer crowds, which might be more prevalent in the fall or spring.

Ultimately, the best time to visit Thunder Bay depends on your preferred activities and the kind of experience you seek. Whether you're drawn to the warm embrace of summer, the vibrant colors of fall, the enchantment of winter, or the awakening of spring, Thunder Bay welcomes you with open arms throughout the year.

Getting There and Around

Embarking on your Thunder Bay adventure involves thoughtful planning on how to reach this captivating destination and seamlessly navigate its diverse offerings. Here's your comprehensive guide to getting there and making the most of your exploration within the city.

Getting to Thunder Bay

By Air

Thunder Bay International Airport (YQT) serves as the gateway for air travelers. It offers direct flights from major Canadian cities and connecting flights from international destinations. Upon arrival, you'll find convenient transportation options to take you into the heart of Thunder Bay.

By Car

For a scenic road trip, Thunder Bay is accessible by car. If you're driving from Toronto, the journey takes approximately 16 hours, offering opportunities to witness the changing landscapes of Ontario. The Trans-Canada Highway provides a direct route to Thunder Bay.

By Bus

Intercity bus services connect Thunder Bay to other major cities in Ontario. Consider this option for a budget-friendly and eco-conscious travel experience. Bus terminals are centrally located, facilitating easy access to the city.

Around Thunder Bay

Public Transit

Thunder Bay Transit operates a comprehensive bus system that covers various neighborhoods and attractions within the city. Bus routes are well-connected, providing an efficient way to explore different parts of Thunder Bay. Check the schedule and routes to plan your city travels.

Car Rentals

To enhance your mobility and explore Thunder Bay at your own pace, car rentals are readily available. Several rental companies provide a variety of vehicles tailored to meet your requirements. Having a car allows you to venture beyond the city center and discover the outskirts and hidden gems.

Taxi Services

Taxis are a convenient option for quick and direct transportation within Thunder Bay. Whether you need to reach a specific attraction or navigate to your accommodation, taxis offer flexibility and door-to-door service.

Cycling

Thunder Bay is a bike-friendly city with dedicated bike lanes and scenic trails. Rent a bike or bring your own to explore the city on two wheels. Cycling not only allows you to enjoy the fresh air but also provides a unique perspective of Thunder Bay's beauty.

Walking

Discover Thunder Bay's charm on foot by exploring its pedestrian-friendly streets. Many attractions, shops, and dining options are within walking distance of the city center. Stroll along the waterfront or through vibrant neighborhoods to absorb the local atmosphere.

Considerations for Your Travel

- Travel Preferences: Choose the mode of transportation that aligns with your preferences for comfort, convenience, and environmental impact.
- Itinerary Planning: Plan your transportation based on your itinerary. If you have specific attractions or activities in mind, consider the most suitable mode of transport for each.
- Local Insights: Engage with locals or consult your accommodation for insights into the best ways to get around hidden gems and transportation tips.

Thus, Thunder Bay offers a variety of transportation options to enhance your overall experience.

Where to Stay

Hotels and Resorts

Choosing the right place to stay in Thunder Bay is an essential part of curating a memorable experience. From cozy retreats to luxurious resorts, the city offers a range of accommodation options to suit every traveler's preferences and budget. Here's a detailed look at some noteworthy places to stay in Thunder Bay:

Delta Hotels by Marriott Thunder Bay

Location: 2240 Sleeping Giant Parkway, Thunder Bay, ON P7A 0E7, Canada

Overlooking the stunning Sleeping Giant Provincial Park, Delta Hotels by Marriott Thunder Bay combines comfort with breathtaking views. The hotel features modern amenities, an indoor pool, and an on-site restaurant serving local and international cuisine. Cost: Starting from $150 per night.

Valhalla Inn

Location: 1 Valhalla Inn Road, Thunder Bay, ON P7E 6J1, Canada

Nestled in a peaceful setting, Valhalla Inn offers a blend of tranquility and convenience. With spacious rooms, a fitness center, and a renowned on-site restaurant, this hotel provides a comfortable retreat. The location provides easy access to the airport and attractions. Cost: Starting from $120 per night.

Prince Arthur Waterfront Hotel & Suites

Location: 17 Cumberland St N, Thunder Bay, ON P7A 4K8, Canada

Situated in the heart of Thunder Bay's waterfront district, Prince Arthur offers historic charm combined with modern comforts. Enjoy views of Lake Superior, explore nearby attractions, and unwind in well-appointed rooms. The hotel's rooftop lounge is a popular spot for panoramic views. Cost: Starting from $130 per night.

Best Western Plus Nor'Wester Hotel & Conference Centre

Location: 2080 Highway #61, Thunder Bay, ON P7J 1B8, Canada

Embrace nature at this hotel nestled within Nor'Wester Mountains. Best Western Plus offers spacious rooms, an indoor pool, and outdoor activities like hiking trails. The on-site restaurant serves local specialties. Cost: Starting from $110 per night.

The Courthouse Hotel

Location: 201 S. Syndicate Ave, Thunder Bay, ON P7E 6V1, Canada

A boutique hotel with a unique character, The Courthouse Hotel is housed in a historic building. Each room is individually designed, showcasing a blend of heritage and contemporary styles. The central location provides easy access to attractions and dining. Cost: Starting from $160 per night.

Days Inn & Suites by Wyndham Thunder Bay

Location: 645 Sibley Dr, Thunder Bay, ON P7B 6Z8, Canada

Ideal for budget-conscious travelers, Days Inn & Suites offers comfortable accommodations with convenient amenities. The hotel features a fitness center, complimentary breakfast, and easy access to the Thunder Bay International Airport. Cost: Starting from $90 per night.

Airlane Hotel and Conference Centre

Location: 698 Arthur Street West, Thunder Bay, ON P7E 5R8, Canada

Airlane Hotel offers a blend of affordability and comfort. With spacious rooms, an indoor pool, and an on-site restaurant, it caters to both leisure and business travelers. The hotel's conference facilities make it suitable for events. Cost: Starting from $80 per night.

TownePlace Suites by Marriott Thunder Bay

Location: 550 Harbour Expressway, Thunder Bay, ON P7E 6P4, Canada

Designed for extended stays, TownePlace Suites offers apartment-style accommodations with fully equipped kitchens. Enjoy the convenience of a fitness center, complimentary breakfast, and proximity to shopping and dining options. Cost: Starting from $140 per night.

These accommodation options provide a spectrum of choices for your stay in Thunder Bay. Whether you seek luxury, historical charm, or budget-friendly comfort, each hotel offers a unique experience, contributing to the overall tapestry of your Thunder

Bay adventure. Prices may vary based on availability, booking dates, and room preferences.

Villas

For those seeking a more secluded and luxurious retreat, Thunder Bay offers a selection of villas that combine comfort with privacy. Whether you're planning a romantic getaway or a family escape, these villas provide a serene haven amidst the stunning natural beauty of Canada's untamed north.

Villa Serenity on Superior

Location: Lake Superior

Perched on the shores of Lake Superior, Villa Serenity offers unparalleled views of the expansive lake. This secluded villa features spacious living areas, private beach access, and outdoor spaces for soaking in the tranquility. Ideal for couples or small groups seeking a serene escape. Cost: Starting from $300 per night.

Northern Oasis Retreat

Location: Thunder Bay District

Tucked away in the Thunder Bay District, Northern Oasis Retreat provides a luxurious escape surrounded by nature. This villa boasts modern amenities, a private hot tub, and panoramic views of the surrounding wilderness. Perfect for those looking for a blend of comfort and seclusion. Cost: Starting from $400 per night.

Superior Pines Villa

Location: Sleeping Giant Provincial Park

Nestled near the iconic Sleeping Giant Provincial Park, Superior Pines Villa offers a unique blend of luxury and natural beauty. The villa features upscale furnishings, a fireplace, and expansive windows for capturing breathtaking views. A haven for nature enthusiasts. Cost: Starting from $350 per night.

Lakeside Tranquility Estate

Location: Loon Lake

This exclusive Lakeside Tranquility Estate is situated on the shores of Loon Lake, providing a secluded escape. The villa comes complete with a private dock, spacious decks, and well-appointed interiors. Perfect for families or groups looking for a lakeside retreat. Cost: Starting from $500 per night.

Majestic Woods Villa

Location: Nor'Wester Mountains

Embrace the beauty of Thunder Bay's Nor'Wester Mountains at Majestic Woods Villa. With luxurious furnishings, an outdoor sauna, and hiking trails at your doorstep, this villa offers a perfect blend of elegance and adventure. A perfect option for individuals in search of a mountain getaway. Cost: Starting from $450 per night.

Harbourview Hideaway

Location: Thunder Bay Waterfront

Overlooking Thunder Bay's waterfront, Harbourview Hideaway provides a sophisticated urban escape. The villa features contemporary design, a private terrace, and proximity to the city's attractions. A perfect choice for those desiring luxury with a cityscape backdrop. Cost: Starting from $380 per night.

Thunder Bay Travel Guide 2024

Tranquil Forest Haven

Location: Thunder Bay Outskirts

Escape to the Tranquil Forest Haven on the outskirts of Thunder Bay. Surrounded by lush forests, this villa offers a peaceful retreat with modern amenities, hiking trails, and a serene atmosphere. Ideal for those seeking seclusion without compromising on comfort. Cost: Starting from $320 per night.

Indulge in the luxury and seclusion of these villas, each providing a unique experience in the heart of Thunder Bay's untamed natural beauty. Prices may vary based on the season, amenities, and booking details, offering a range of options for those looking to elevate their Thunder Bay experience.

Guesthouses and Bed & Breakfasts

For a more intimate and personalized stay, Thunder Bay offers an array of guesthouses and bed and breakfasts (B&Bs). These accommodations provide a cozy atmosphere, warm hospitality, and a chance to connect with the local community. Immerse yourself in Thunder Bay's charm by considering these delightful guesthouses and B&Bs:

Hillcrest Guest House

Location: 132 Hillcrest Dr, Thunder Bay, ON P7B 1T6, Canada

Nestled in a quiet neighborhood, Hillcrest Guest House offers a peaceful retreat with comfortable rooms and a homey ambiance. Guests can enjoy a hearty homemade breakfast and personalized attention from the hosts. Conveniently located near local attractions. Cost: Starting from $90 per night.

Alderwood B&B

Location: 222 Alderwood Dr, Thunder Bay, ON P7C 1G4, Canada

Alderwood B&B provides a charming escape surrounded by nature. The cozy rooms, adorned with unique decor, create a homely atmosphere. Guests can savor a delicious breakfast, including homemade treats. The B&B is situated close to outdoor trails and parks. Cost: Starting from $100 per night.

Ellis House Bed & Breakfast

Location: 1000 E. Frederica St, Thunder Bay, ON P7E 3V9, Canada

Ellis House, a historic bed and breakfast, offers elegant accommodations with a touch of Victorian charm. Guests can enjoy well-appointed rooms, a garden terrace, and a delightful breakfast prepared with locally sourced ingredients. Conveniently located near the city center. Cost: Starting from $120 per night.

A Touch of Ginger Bed and Breakfast

Location: 19 Shuniah St, Thunder Bay, ON P7A 2Y9, Canada

A Touch of Ginger is a cozy bed and breakfast with uniquely decorated rooms and personalized touches. Guests can indulge in a gourmet breakfast and relax in the inviting common areas. The B&B is within walking distance of waterfront attractions. Cost: Starting from $110 per night.

Pine Cottage B&B

Location: 825 Lakeshore Dr, Thunder Bay, ON P7A 1A1, Canada

Pine Cottage B&B offers a lakeside retreat with a rustic charm. The comfortable rooms, adorned with wooden furnishings, provide a cozy ambiance. Guests can enjoy a delicious breakfast while overlooking the scenic surroundings. Ideal for those seeking a lakeside escape. Cost: Starting from $95 per night.

Morningstar Cottage Bed & Breakfast

Location: 1032 Lakeshore Dr, Thunder Bay, ON P7A 0P3, Canada

Nestled along Lake Superior, Morningstar Cottage B&B provides a tranquil setting with well-appointed rooms. Guests can start their day with a homemade breakfast while enjoying lake views. The B&B is a short drive from Thunder Bay's attractions. Cost: Starting from $130 per night.

Pearl Street Guesthouse

Location: 828 Pearl St, Thunder Bay, ON P7B 1M7, Canada

Pearl Street Guesthouse offers a cozy and welcoming atmosphere in the heart of Thunder Bay. Guests can unwind in comfortable rooms and enjoy a continental breakfast. The guesthouse is conveniently located near downtown shops and restaurants. Cost: Starting from $85 per night.

These guesthouses and B&Bs provide a warm and personalized experience, allowing you to connect with Thunder Bay's hospitality while enjoying comfortable accommodations. Prices may vary based on room selection, amenities, and booking details, offering a range of options for those seeking a more intimate stay.

Budget-Friendly Accommodations

Travelers seeking budget-friendly accommodations in Thunder Bay can find a variety of options that balance affordability with comfort. From hostels to budget hotels, these establishments provide a wallet-friendly stay while ensuring you can make the most of your Thunder Bay adventure. Here are some recommendations for those mindful of their travel budget:

Thunder Bay International Hostel

Location: 141 Elm St S, Thunder Bay, ON P7B 3J3, Canada

Thunder Bay International Hostel offers budget-conscious travelers a shared accommodation experience. With dormitory-style rooms, communal spaces, and a friendly atmosphere, it's an excellent choice for solo travelers or those seeking a social environment. Cost: Starting from $30 per night.

Econo Lodge Thunder Bay

Location: 686 Memorial Ave, Thunder Bay, ON P7B 3Z5, Canada

Econo Lodge Thunder Bay provides affordable rooms with essential amenities. Located near the Thunder Bay International Airport, it's a convenient choice for budget travelers. The hotel offers complimentary breakfast and easy access to local attractions. Cost: Starting from $70 per night.

Super 8 by Wyndham Thunder Bay

Location: 439 Memorial Ave, Thunder Bay, ON P7B 3Y6, Canada

Super 8 by Wyndham Thunder Bay offers budget-friendly rooms with practical amenities. Guests can enjoy a complimentary breakfast and take advantage of the hotel's convenient location for exploring Thunder Bay. Ideal for those seeking affordability without compromising on comfort. Cost: Starting from $80 per night.

Days Inn by Wyndham Thunder Bay North

Location: 1250 Golf Links Rd, Thunder Bay, ON P7B 7A4, Canada

Days Inn Thunder Bay North provides budget accommodations with a focus on comfort. Guests can enjoy amenities such as an indoor pool and complimentary breakfast. The hotel is situated near various dining options and attractions. Cost: Starting from $85 per night.

Motel 6 Thunder Bay

Location: 666 W Arthur St, Thunder Bay, ON P7E 5R8, Canada

Motel 6 Thunder Bay offers straightforward and affordable rooms for budget-conscious travelers. The motel provides essential amenities, including pet-friendly options, making it suitable for a range of travelers. Conveniently located near Thunder Bay International Airport. Cost: Starting from $60 per night.

A&K Motel

Location: 1421 Dawson Rd, Thunder Bay, ON P7G 1H9, Canada

A&K Motel offers budget-friendly rooms in a relaxed setting. With simple accommodations and practical amenities, it caters to travelers seeking affordability. The location of the motel provides convenient access to local attractions. Cost: Starting from $50 per night.

Kangaroo Inn

Location: 1219 E. Frederica St, Thunder Bay, ON P7E 3V3, Canada

Kangaroo Inn provides affordable and clean accommodations for budget travelers. With a range of room options, it caters to various preferences. The inn's location offers proximity to Thunder Bay's attractions and dining options. Cost: Starting from $55 per night.

These budget-friendly accommodations in Thunder Bay ensure that you can enjoy a comfortable stay without exceeding your travel budget. Prices may vary based on room selection, availability, and booking details, providing options for those seeking cost-effective accommodations.

Budgeting for your Trip

Embarking on a memorable journey to Thunder Bay doesn't mean breaking the bank. With thoughtful planning and budgeting, you can make the most of your adventure without compromising on experiences. Here's a practical guide to help you budget wisely for your trip to Canada's untamed north:

Accommodations

Hostels and Budget Hotels: Consider staying in budget-friendly hostels or hotels. Options like Thunder Bay International Hostel, Econo Lodge, or Motel 6 provide affordable stays without compromising on comfort.

Comparison Shopping: Use online platforms to compare prices and read reviews. Booking in advance can often secure better deals.

Transportation

Public Transit: Explore Thunder Bay using the local transit system. It's a cost-effective way to navigate the city and reach popular attractions.

Car Rentals: If you plan to venture into the surrounding wilderness, renting a car can offer flexibility. Compare pricing options across various rental agencies to discover the most favorable offer.

Dining

Local Eateries: Enjoy the flavors of Thunder Bay at local eateries and food markets. Look for budget-friendly options like food trucks and casual diners.

Grocery Stores: Save on meals by picking up snacks and easy-to-prepare items from grocery stores.

Activities and Attractions

Free and Low-Cost Activities: Take advantage of Thunder Bay's natural beauty with activities like hiking and exploring parks. Many attractions offer free or low-cost admission on certain days.

Package Deals: Look for bundled tickets or passes that include multiple attractions at a discounted rate.

Entertainment

Local Events: Check out local event calendars for free or low-cost cultural events, festivals, or live performances happening during your visit.

Outdoor Recreation: Explore Thunder Bay's outdoor offerings, such as hiking trails and parks, which often come with minimal or no cost.

Transportation to Thunder Bay

Flight Deals: Monitor flight prices and consider flexible dates. Booking during off-peak times or midweek can often result in lower airfares.

Travel Packages: Explore vacation packages that bundle flights and accommodations for potential savings.

Souvenirs and Shopping

Local Markets: Shop for souvenirs at local markets or artisan stalls for unique and budget-friendly finds.

Set a Souvenir Budget: Determine a specific budget for souvenirs to avoid overspending.

Miscellaneous Expenses

Travel Insurance: While it's an additional expense, having travel insurance can save you money in case of unexpected events.

Emergency Fund: Set aside a small amount as an emergency fund for unexpected expenses.

By planning and being mindful of your spending, you can create a budget that allows you to savor the best of Thunder Bay without financial stress. Remember to allocate funds based on your priorities, whether it's exploring natural wonders, trying local cuisine, or immersing yourself in cultural experiences. Safe travels and enjoy your budget-friendly adventure in Thunder Bay!

Chapter 1

Itineraries: 3-Day

Action-Packed Adventure

Day 1: Embrace the Wilderness

Your Thunder Bay adventure kicks off with an exhilarating 3-day itinerary that immerses you in the heart of nature. On Day 1, set the tone by embracing the untamed wilderness that defines Thunder Bay.

Morning: Hike the Sleeping Giant

Rise with the sun and lace up your hiking boots for an early morning trek to the iconic Sleeping Giant. The trails range from strolls to challenging hikes, offering panoramic views of Lake Superior. Feel the crisp morning air as you traverse the rugged terrain, with the Sleeping Giant formation towering above, creating a dramatic backdrop.

Afternoon: Kayak Lake Superior

As the day unfolds, transition to the tranquil waters of Lake Superior. Grab a kayak and paddle along the shoreline, immersing yourself in the vastness of the world's largest freshwater lake. The crystal-clear waters reveal the hidden beauty beneath, making every stroke a journey into the heart of Thunder Bay's natural wonders.

Evening: Sunset at Hillcrest Park

Wrap up your day with a visit to Hillcrest Park, a vantage point that offers a breathtaking view of Thunder Bay and Lake Superior.

As the sun begins its descent, the sky transforms into a canvas of colors, casting a warm glow over the city. This serene setting provides the perfect backdrop for reflection and appreciation of Thunder Bay's unspoiled beauty.

Day 2: Outdoor Excitement

On Day 2, delve deeper into Thunder Bay's outdoor allure, with a focus on thrilling activities that will leave you invigorated.

Morning: Cycling Adventure

Start your day with an invigorating cycling adventure. Thunder Bay boasts scenic bike paths and routes suitable for various skill levels. Whether you prefer a leisurely ride along the waterfront or a more challenging mountain biking trail, the city caters to cyclists of all preferences.

Afternoon: Blue Point Amethyst Mine

For a unique and interactive experience, head to the Blue Point Amethyst Mine. Spend your afternoon digging for your very own amethyst treasures. The mine offers an opportunity to connect with Thunder Bay's geological wonders, leaving you with a tangible and sparkling souvenir of your adventure.

Evening: Lakeside Dining

As the day winds down, treat yourself to a lakeside dining experience. Thunder Bay is home to a variety of restaurants offering fresh local seafood and international cuisine. Enjoy a delicious meal while overlooking Lake Superior, savoring both the flavors on your plate and the scenic beauty surrounding you.

Day 3: Cultural Exploration

Conclude your 3-day adventure with a focus on Thunder Bay's rich history and cultural tapestry, providing a deeper understanding of the region's past.

Morning: Fort William Historical Park

Begin your day with a journey back in time at Fort William Historical Park. Explore the reconstructed fur trading post, engaging with costumed interpreters who bring the history of the fur trade era to life. The immersive experience offers insights into Thunder Bay's role in shaping Canada's early economic landscape.

Afternoon: Indigenous Culture Discovery

Immerse yourself in Thunder Bay's vibrant Indigenous culture by visiting museums, and art galleries, and attending traditional events. Gain a deeper appreciation for the customs, traditions, and artistic expressions that have shaped the region. Thunder Bay's Indigenous heritage adds a layer of cultural richness to your adventure.

Evening: Culinary Delights

Conclude your 3-day journey with a culinary exploration of Thunder Bay's diverse flavors. Indulge in local delicacies, from Indigenous-inspired dishes to international cuisine. Choose a restaurant that resonates with your taste buds, providing a delicious end to your Thunder Bay adventure.

As you reflect on your 3-day action-packed adventure, you'll carry with you not only memories of stunning landscapes and thrilling activities but also a profound connection to the untamed north of

Canada. Thunder Bay, with its natural beauty and cultural depth, beckons you to return for more explorations in the future.

Family Fun Weekend

Day 1: Nature's Playground

Embark on a family-friendly weekend in Thunder Bay, immersing your loved ones in a blend of nature and excitement.

Morning: Wildlife Exploration at Centennial Park

Start your day with a visit to Centennial Park, a haven for nature enthusiasts of all ages. Stroll along the trails, keeping an eye out for the diverse bird species that call the park home. Engage your family in a friendly bird-watching challenge, fostering an appreciation for the region's natural inhabitants.

Afternoon: Picnic and Play at Chippewa Park

Transition to Chippewa Park for a delightful afternoon of family bonding. Set up a picnic by the shores of Lake Superior, indulging in local treats and enjoying the scenic views. The park's playgrounds and open spaces offer ample opportunities for the kids to burn off energy, ensuring smiles and laughter throughout.

Evening: Sunset Cruise on the Kam River

Wrap up the day with a family-friendly sunset cruise on the Kam River. Board a boat and cruise along the tranquil waters as the sun paints the sky with hues of orange and pink. It's a magical experience for both adults and children, creating lasting memories against the backdrop of Thunder Bay's natural beauty.

Day 2: Aquatic Adventures

Dive into aquatic adventures that cater to every family member's sense of fun and exploration.

Morning: Aquatic Center and Water Slides

Kick off the day with a visit to Thunder Bay's Aquatic Center, a water wonderland for the whole family. Enjoy the excitement of water slides, splash pads, and a lazy river. The center provides a perfect blend of relaxation and thrills, ensuring everyone in the family has a splashing good time.

Afternoon: Kayaking on Boulevard Lake

For a more serene water experience, head to Boulevard Lake for a family kayaking adventure. Navigate through the serene waters, absorbing the scenic beauty of the surroundings. This activity allows families to bond while appreciating Thunder Bay's natural beauty from a unique perspective.

Evening: Lakeside Barbecue at Marina Park

Cap off the day with a lakeside barbecue at Marina Park. Gather around a fire pit, roast marshmallows, and enjoy a family-friendly barbecue. The park's open spaces provide an ideal setting for a relaxed evening by Lake Superior, allowing your family to unwind and share stories under the starlit sky.

Day 3: Cultural Connections

Wrap up your family's fun weekend with a touch of culture, creating a well-rounded and enriching experience for everyone.

Morning: Thunder Bay Art Gallery

Begin the day with a visit to the Thunder Bay Art Gallery. Explore vibrant exhibits that showcase the talents of local and Indigenous artists. Engage the family in interactive activities and workshops, allowing everyone to express their creativity.

Afternoon: Family-Friendly Dining Downtown

Head to Thunder Bay's downtown area for a family-friendly dining experience. Choose from a variety of restaurants that cater to all tastes, providing a perfect setting for a leisurely family lunch. Take a stroll through the downtown streets, discovering local shops and perhaps indulging in some ice cream treats.

Evening: Movie Night at SilverCity Thunder Bay

Conclude your family's fun weekend with a cozy movie night at Silver City Thunder Bay. Choose a family-friendly film and enjoy a relaxed evening at the cinema. It's a perfect way to wind down while sharing laughs and creating lasting memories with your loved ones.

As your family bids farewell to Thunder Bay, you'll carry with you the joyous echoes of laughter, the beauty of shared experiences, and the warmth of a weekend filled with family fun. Thunder Bay, with its diverse offerings, welcomes families to create bonds that last a lifetime amidst the backdrop of Canada's untamed north.

Romantic Getaway for Two

Day 1: Serenity and Scenic Strolls

Embark on a romantic escape in Thunder Bay, designed to ignite sparks and create intimate memories for you and your partner.

Morning: Lakeside Breakfast at The Hoito

Begin your romantic getaway with a lakeside breakfast at The Hoito, a charming Finnish restaurant. Indulge in delectable dishes while overlooking Lake Superior, setting the tone for a day of shared moments.

Late Morning: Botanical Gardens and Conservatory

Stroll hand in hand through the beautiful Centennial Botanical Conservatory and Gardens. The vibrant blooms and fragrant flowers create a serene atmosphere, providing the perfect backdrop for quiet conversations and stolen kisses.

Afternoon: Gourmet Picnic at Trowbridge Falls

Escape to the picturesque Trowbridge Falls Park for a gourmet picnic. Pack a basket with your favorite treats and find a secluded spot by the falls. The soothing sound of cascading water and the natural beauty surrounding you create a romantic ambiance.

Evening: Sunset Dinner Cruise on Lake Superior

As the sun begins to set, embark on a sunset dinner cruise on Lake Superior. Cruise along the pristine waters, savoring a gourmet meal with your loved one. The breathtaking sunset paints the sky in hues of pink and gold, providing a romantic backdrop to your evening.

Day 2: Secluded Adventures

Continue your romantic escape with secluded adventures that bring you closer together.

Morning: Private Kayaking Experience

Embark on a private kayaking experience on one of Thunder Bay's serene lakes. Paddle together, exploring hidden coves and enjoying the tranquility of nature. The shared experience fosters a sense of closeness and intimacy.

Afternoon: Couples' Spa Retreat

Indulge in a couples' spa retreat at one of Thunder Bay's wellness centers. Relax and rejuvenate with massages, spa treatments, and a tranquil atmosphere. The spa provides an intimate setting for you and your partner to unwind and connect on a deeper level.

Evening: Fine Dining at Caribou Restaurant

Conclude your day with a romantic dinner at Caribou Restaurant, known for its intimate ambiance and exquisite cuisine. Enjoy a culinary journey together, savoring dishes made with locally sourced ingredients. The cozy atmosphere and attentive service create a perfect setting for a romantic evening.

Day 3: Scenic Views and Shared Moments

Wrap up your romantic getaway with breathtaking views and cherished shared moments.

Morning: Sunrise at Mount McKay

Start your day early with a visit to Mount McKay for a breathtaking sunrise experience. The panoramic views of Thunder Bay and Lake Superior bathed in morning light create a magical atmosphere. Capture the moment with your partner as you witness the world awakening.

Late Morning: Coffee Date at Bay Village Coffee

Head to Bay Village Coffee for a leisurely late-morning coffee date. This charming café offers a cozy setting, allowing you to reflect on your romantic escape and savor the last moments of your time together in Thunder Bay.

As you bid farewell to Thunder Bay, your hearts will carry the echoes of laughter, the warmth of shared experiences, and the magic of a romantic getaway that lingers long after your journey. Thunder Bay, with its natural beauty and secluded charm, provides an idyllic backdrop for couples seeking an intimate escape in Canada's untamed north.

Solo Explorer's Journey

Day 1: Nature's Solitude

Embark on a solo exploration of Thunder Bay, immersing yourself in the natural wonders and tranquility that define this untamed northern city.

Morning: Sunrise at Mission Island Marsh

Start your journey with the serenity of a sunrise at Mission Island Marsh. As the sun bathes the marsh in golden hues, you'll find a peaceful haven to reflect and embrace the solitude of the early morning.

Late Morning: Agate Beach Discovery

Head to Agate Beach, known for its unique collection of agate stones. The rhythmic sound of Lake Superior's waves and the thrill of finding hidden treasures create a calming yet adventurous start to your solo expedition.

Afternoon: Exploration at Ouimet Canyon

Venture to Ouimet Canyon, a majestic natural wonder with breathtaking views. The solitude of this geological masterpiece allows for introspection and connection with the raw beauty of Thunder Bay's wilderness.

Evening: Sunset at Silver Islet

Cap off your day with a sunset visit to Silver Islet. Perched on the shores of Lake Superior, this historic village offers a quiet retreat where you can absorb the colors of the setting sun, casting a warm glow over the landscape.

Day 2: Personal Discoveries

Continue your solo journey with activities designed for personal discovery and a deeper connection with Thunder Bay.

Morning: Independent Hike in Sleeping Giant Provincial Park

Embark on an independent hike in Sleeping Giant Provincial Park. Choose a trail that resonates with your spirit, whether it's a challenging ascent or a stroll. The park's diverse landscapes provide a canvas for self-reflection amidst the beauty of nature.

Afternoon: Artistic Inspiration at Thunder Bay Art Gallery

Visit the Thunder Bay Art Gallery for a solo exploration of artistic expression. Engage with thought-provoking exhibits and allow the diverse artworks to inspire your reflections. The gallery becomes a sanctuary for solo travelers seeking cultural enrichment.

Evening: Riverside Dinner at Nook Thunder Bay

Dine solo at Nook Thunder Bay, a riverside restaurant with a relaxed atmosphere. Enjoy a flavorful meal while watching the gentle flow of the river—a perfect setting for introspection and appreciation of Thunder Bay's unique charm.

Day 3: City Unveiling

Conclude your solo journey by delving into Thunder Bay's urban offerings, providing a dynamic contrast to the solitude of nature.

Morning: Coffee and Exploration in the Waterfront District

Begin your day with a solo exploration of Thunder Bay's Waterfront District. Grab a coffee from one of the local cafes and meander through the vibrant streets, discovering boutiques, art galleries, and the dynamic energy of the city.

Afternoon: Fort William Historical Park Exploration

Immerse yourself in history at Fort William Historical Park. Wander through the reconstructed fur trading post, absorbing the tales of the past. The immersive experience offers a solo traveler a unique connection with Thunder Bay's historical tapestry.

Evening: Reflective Dinner at The Foundry

Conclude your solo adventure with a reflective dinner at The Foundry. This chic restaurant provides a sophisticated yet relaxed atmosphere for solo diners. Savor a delicious meal while pondering the memories and personal discoveries made during your solo journey in Thunder Bay.

As you bid adieu to Thunder Bay, you'll carry with you the echoes of nature's solitude, the inspiration of personal discoveries, and the unique charm of a city that offers both quiet retreats and dynamic urban experiences. Thunder Bay, with its blend of natural beauty and cultural depth, invites solo explorers to embark on a journey of self-discovery in Canada's untamed north.

Chapter 2

Family-Friendly Travel

Kid-Approved Activities & Attractions

Thunder Bay opens its arms wide to families seeking unforgettable adventures. In the realm of family-friendly travel, Thunder Bay stands out as a playground for young explorers. Here, every step is a discovery, and every sight is a marvel. Let's delve into the kid-approved activities and attractions that will have your little ones buzzing with excitement.

Lake Superior's Maritime Marvels

Dock your family's adventure at the shores of Lake Superior, the expansive freshwater giant that sets the stage for maritime wonders. The Thunder Bay waterfront is a hub of family-friendly activities, offering a blend of recreation and education. The thrilling adventures at the marina, including boat tours and scenic cruises, capture the imagination of young sailors. Set sail on these kid-friendly excursions, where the tales of the lake come alive, weaving stories of exploration and discovery.

Chutes and Ladders at Centennial Park

Centennial Park, a haven for family fun, presents a delightful combination of green spaces and engaging activities. Watch as your kids climb and conquer the play structures resembling treehouse wonders. The park's expansive grounds are perfect for picnics and strolls. Let the little ones loose on the playground's chutes and ladders, fostering a sense of adventure and accomplishment.

A Walk on the Wild Side at Thunder Bay Zoo

For an immersive wildlife experience, the Thunder Bay Zoo awaits, inviting young minds to connect with the wonders of the animal kingdom. Wander through themed exhibits that showcase a diverse array of species. From majestic lions to playful lemurs, the zoo provides an educational and entertaining experience for children of all ages. Engage in hands-on activities and witness the joy on your kids' faces as they interact with the inhabitants of this wildlife sanctuary.

Science and Exploration at Science North

Fuel the curiosity of budding scientists at Thunder Bay's Science North. This interactive science center transforms learning into a thrilling adventure. Watch as your little ones experiment with hands-on exhibits, engaging in activities that make scientific principles come to life. From the wonders of space to the secrets of the deep sea, Science North sparks a passion for exploration, leaving your kids with a newfound appreciation for the world around them.

Journey Through Time at the Thunder Bay Museum

Step into the past with a visit to the Thunder Bay Museum, where history unfolds in captivating displays. Wander through exhibits that transport your family to different eras, from the fur trade days to the industrial boom. The museum's kid-friendly sections ensure that history becomes an exciting journey rather than a distant tale. Interactive displays and engaging artifacts make learning about Thunder Bay's rich history an adventure for the entire family.

Nature's Playground at Cascades Conservation Area

Immerse your family in the wonders of nature at Cascades Conservation Area. A haven for outdoor enthusiasts, this area combines scenic beauty with activities suitable for all ages. Take a leisurely hike along family-friendly trails, letting your kids discover the magic of the wilderness. The cascading waterfalls provide a breathtaking backdrop, offering a perfect setting for family picnics and exploration. Dip your toes into the crystal-clear waters, creating memories that will last a lifetime.

Artistic Adventures at Definitely Superior Art Gallery

Nurture the creative spirits of your little artists at the Definitely Superior Art Gallery. This cultural gem introduces children to the world of contemporary art through visually stimulating exhibits. Participate in art activities suitable for families, promoting self-expression and imagination. The gallery's vibrant atmosphere sparks curiosity, making it an ideal destination for families seeking a blend of culture and creativity.

Sweet Sensations at Hoito Restaurant

Cap off your family-friendly adventures with a visit to the iconic Hoito Restaurant, a Thunder Bay institution that has been serving delicious meals since 1918. Indulge in Finnish pancakes and other comfort foods that cater to the tastes of both young and adult palates. The warm and welcoming atmosphere makes it an ideal spot for families to share stories of their Thunder Bay escapades.

Thus, Thunder Bay's family-friendly offerings extend far beyond the ordinary. From maritime marvels to artistic adventures, each attraction is designed to captivate the young minds of your explorers. Let Thunder Bay become the backdrop for unforgettable family moments, where laughter echoes through Centennial Park, the roar of lions resonates at the zoo, and the wonders of science come alive at Science North. Your family's journey in Thunder Bay is not just a trip; it's a collection of magical moments waiting to be discovered.

Family-Friendly Accommodation & Dining

Family-Friendly Accommodation

Valhalla Inn

Location: 1 Valhalla Inn Road, Thunder Bay, ON P7E 6J1

Cost: Starting at $120 per night

Nestled in a serene setting, Valhalla Inn offers family-friendly accommodations with spacious rooms and amenities such as a pool and play area. Conveniently located near Thunder Bay International Airport, it provides easy access to family attractions.

Hampton Inn & Suites by Hilton Thunder Bay

Location: 760 Arthur St W, Thunder Bay, ON P7E 5R9

Cost: Starting at $130 per night

Situated in the heart of Thunder Bay, Hampton Inn & Suites combines comfort and convenience. Family suites are available, and the hotel offers complimentary breakfast, ensuring a hassle-free start to your family's day of exploration.

Days Inn by Wyndham Thunder Bay North

Location: 1250 Golf Links Rd, Thunder Bay, ON P7B 0A1

Cost: Starting at $90 per night

Days Inn provides budget-friendly accommodation without compromising on comfort. Family rooms are available, and the location offers proximity to various family attractions, making it a practical choice for your Thunder Bay adventure.

Best Western Plus Nor'Wester Hotel & Conference Centre

Location: 2080 Highway 61, Thunder Bay, ON P7J 1B8

Cost: Starting at $110 per night

Embrace a tranquil stay at Best Western Plus Nor'Wester, surrounded by nature. Family suites are available, and the hotel's amenities include a pool and on-site dining, providing a relaxing retreat after a day of family adventures.

Victoria Inn Hotel & Convention Centre

Location: 555 Arthur St W, Thunder Bay, ON P7E 5R5

Cost: Starting at $100 per night

Victoria Inn offers family-friendly accommodations with spacious rooms and an indoor pool. Conveniently located near major attractions, it provides a comfortable base for families exploring Thunder Bay.

Holiday Inn Express & Suites Thunder Bay

Location: 1041 Carrick St, Thunder Bay, ON P7B 6L9

Cost: Starting at $110 per night

Experience modern comfort at Holiday Inn Express, offering family suites and complimentary breakfast. Situated close to popular family attractions, it combines convenience with a welcoming atmosphere.

Airlane Hotel & Conference Centre

Location: 698 Arthur St W, Thunder Bay, ON P7E 5R8

Cost: Starting at $95 per night

Airlane Hotel provides family-friendly accommodation with a focus on affordability. With spacious rooms and amenities like a pool, it's an excellent choice for families seeking a budget-friendly stay.

Comfort Inn Thunder Bay

Location: 660 W Arthur St, Thunder Bay, ON P7E 5R8

Cost: Starting at $85 per night

Offering a blend of comfort and value, Comfort Inn Thunder Bay caters to families with affordable rates and convenient amenities. Located near family-friendly attractions, it ensures a pleasant stay for your entire crew.

Family-Friendly Dining

The Keg Steakhouse + Bar

Location: 735 Hewitson St, Thunder Bay, ON P7B 5V5

Cost: Family meals starting at $60

Indulge in a family-friendly dining experience at The Keg, known for its welcoming atmosphere and diverse menu. From sizzling steaks to kid-approved options, this restaurant caters to various tastes within a cozy setting.

Tomlin Restaurant

Location: 202 S Algoma St, Thunder Bay, ON P7B 3C1

Cost: Family meals starting at $50

Tomlin Restaurant offers a blend of contemporary and comfort food, providing a family-friendly environment in the heart of Thunder Bay. The menu includes options for both adults and kids, ensuring a delightful dining experience.

The Madhouse

Location: 508 S Camelot St, Thunder Bay, ON P7E 1P8

Cost: Family meals starting at $40

Dive into a casual and family-friendly atmosphere at The Madhouse. This eatery serves up a variety of comfort foods and offers an extensive menu suitable for all ages. It's a laid-back option for families looking for a relaxed dining experience.

Nook

Location: 499 S Cumberland St, Thunder Bay, ON P7B 2Y3

Cost: Family meals starting at $45

For a cozy and family-friendly dining experience, visit Nook. Known for its warm ambiance and diverse menu, Nook caters to various tastes, making it a suitable choice for families exploring Thunder Bay.

The Silver Birch Restaurant

Location: 28 N Cumberland St, Thunder Bay, ON P7A 4L3

Cost: Family meals starting at $55

Delight in a family-friendly dining experience at The Silver Birch Restaurant. Known for its diverse menu and welcoming ambiance, it provides a relaxed setting for families to enjoy a delicious meal together.

Red Lion Smokehouse

Location: 28 Cumberland St S, Thunder Bay, ON P7B 2T2

Cost: Family meals starting at $50

For families craving a taste of barbecue, Red Lion Smokehouse is the place to be. With a casual atmosphere and a menu that caters to various preferences, it's a hit among both adults and kids.

Boston Pizza

Location: 425 Memorial Ave, Thunder Bay, ON P7B 3Y6

Cost: Family meals starting at $40

Enjoy a family-friendly meal at Boston Pizza, where a diverse menu offers options for every palate. The lively atmosphere and kid-friendly selections make it a favorite among families exploring Thunder Bay.

The Foundry Pub Grub

Location: 242 Red River Rd, Thunder Bay, ON P7B 1A6

Cost: Family meals starting at $45

Experience a blend of pub fare and family-friendly ambiance at The Foundry Pub Grub. With a menu that caters to all ages, it's an ideal spot for families to unwind after a day of exploring Thunder Bay.

Thunder Bay's family-friendly accommodation and dining options are tailored to make your stay memorable. Whether you choose the comfort of Valhalla Inn, the convenience of Hampton Inn & Suites, the budget-friendly Days Inn, or the tranquility of Best Western Plus Nor'Wester, each accommodation option offers a welcoming retreat for your family.

As you explore Thunder Bay, enjoy family meals at The Keg Steakhouse + Bar, Tomlin Restaurant, The Madhouse, and Nook. These dining establishments provide diverse menus, cozy atmospheres, and family-friendly pricing, ensuring that every meal becomes a cherished part of your Thunder Bay adventure.

Outdoor Adventures for the Whole Bunch

Thunder Bay's outdoor wonders extend beyond breathtaking landscapes—there's an abundance of family-friendly adventures waiting to be embraced. Unleash the spirit of exploration as your whole bunch immerses themselves in the diverse outdoor activities that Thunder Bay has to offer.

Kinsmen Park Playground

Location: 515 Grenville Ave, Thunder Bay, ON P7A 2A6

Discover a playground haven at Kinsmen Park, where your little ones can climb, swing, and slide to their hearts' content. Surrounded by green spaces, it's an ideal spot for a family picnic while the kids engage in energetic play.

Trowbridge Falls Park

Location: 600 Carrick St, Thunder Bay, ON P7B 6L9

Embark on a nature-filled day at Trowbridge Falls Park. Hike along the trails suitable for all ages, leading you to the picturesque falls. The whole bunch can enjoy a picnic by the river, creating cherished family memories.

Thunder Bay Country Market

Location: 1080 Windsor St, Thunder Bay, ON P7B 6B9

Immerse your family in the vibrant atmosphere of Thunder Bay Country Market. Stroll through the market, explore local produce, and indulge in tasty treats. It's an outdoor adventure for the senses, where the whole bunch can savor the flavors of Thunder Bay.

Boulevard Lake Park

Location: 650 Boulevard Lake Rd, Thunder Bay, ON P7B 5N3

Engage in a day of outdoor fun at Boulevard Lake Park. Take a leisurely walk or bike ride around the lake, enjoy a family-friendly picnic, and let the kids play at the playground. With scenic views and recreational spaces, it's a delightful spot for the whole family.

Chippewa Park

Location: 2615 City Rd, Thunder Bay, ON P7J 1K7

Dive into a day of adventure at Chippewa Park. From the sandy beaches along Lake Superior to the charming zoo, there's something for everyone. Let the whole bunch explore the playgrounds, splash pad, and walking trails, creating lasting memories in this family-friendly oasis.

Mount McKay Scenic Lookout

Location: 1000 Highway 61, Thunder Bay, ON P7B 5E4

Elevate your family adventure at Mount McKay Scenic Lookout. Drive or hike to the top for panoramic views of Thunder Bay and Lake Superior. It's an outdoor experience that provides a sense of achievement for the whole bunch, accompanied by stunning vistas.

Centennial Park Wildlife Exhibit

Location: 135 S Franklin St, Thunder Bay, ON P7E 1R8

Immerse your family in a unique outdoor adventure at Centennial Park Wildlife Exhibit. Encounter local wildlife in a natural setting, providing an educational and entertaining experience for the whole bunch. It's a chance to connect with Thunder Bay's natural wonders up close.

Mission Island Marsh Conservation Area

Location: 141 S Water St, Thunder Bay, ON P7B 4T9

Explore the wonders of wetlands at Mission Island Marsh Conservation Area. Walk along the boardwalks, observe diverse bird species, and let the whole bunch appreciate the beauty of this natural habitat. It's an outdoor adventure that combines education with the joy of exploration.

Thunder Bay's outdoor adventures cater to the whole bunch, ensuring that families can connect with nature and each other. Embrace the variety of adventures Thunder Bay has to offer, creating a tapestry of outdoor memories for the whole bunch to cherish.

Rainy Day Fun & Educational Activities

Don't let the rain dampen your family's spirits in Thunder Bay. Embrace the cozy side of exploration with a collection of indoor, fun, and educational activities that ensure your family's adventure continues, rain or shine.

Thunder Bay Art Gallery

Location: 1080 Keewatin St, Thunder Bay, ON P7B 6T7

Experience the Arts: On a rainy day, venture into the Thunder Bay Art Gallery. Explore the diverse exhibits showcasing regional and Indigenous art. Engage in interactive displays that provide a glimpse into Thunder Bay's artistic tapestry, making it an educational and visually stimulating indoor activity for the whole family.

Thunder Bay Museum

Location: 425 Donald St E, Thunder Bay, ON P7E 5V1

Time Travel Indoors: Step back in time at the Thunder Bay Museum. Wander through exhibits that unveil the city's history, from its Indigenous roots to the industrial era. Rainy days provide the perfect backdrop for an educational journey through Thunder Bay's past, creating an enriching experience for the whole family.

Crock-N-Dial Indoor Mini Golf

Location: 405 S Waterloo St, Thunder Bay, ON P7E 2M4

Mini Golf Extravaganza: Turn a rainy day into a mini-golf adventure at Crock-N-Dial. This indoor mini-golf facility offers a whimsical and family-friendly setting. Navigate through creative courses, bringing laughter and friendly competition to your family's indoor escapade.

The Exploration Studio

Location: 183 W Algoma St, Thunder Bay, ON P7B 3C1

Hands-On Learning: Fuel your family's curiosity at The Exploration Studio. Engage in hands-on educational activities that blend science and creativity. From interactive exhibits to workshops, it's a haven for rainy days where learning becomes a thrilling adventure.

In Common

Location: 207 E Miles St, Thunder Bay, ON P7E 1H6

Community-Centric Creativity: On rainy days, seek refuge at In Common, a community-focused creative space. Participate in family-friendly workshops, art classes, and cultural events that nurture both creativity and a sense of community. It's an indoor hub where your family can connect with Thunder Bay's vibrant local culture.

Intercity Shopping Centre

Location: 1000 Fort William Rd, Thunder Bay, ON P7B 6B9

Retail Therapy and More: Embrace retail therapy and family fun at Intercity Shopping Centre. Beyond shopping, this indoor destination offers entertainment options, including a play area for kids. Spend a rainy day exploring shops, enjoying meals, and engaging in family-friendly activities under one roof.

SilverCity Thunder Bay Cinemas

Location: 850 N May St, Thunder Bay, ON P7C 6A5

Cinematic Adventures: When the rain falls, venture into SilverCity Thunder Bay Cinemas. Experience the magic of the big screen with family-friendly movie options. Rainy days become cinematic adventures, providing entertainment and shared moments for the whole family.

OLG Casino Thunder Bay

Location: 50 Cumberland St S, Thunder Bay, ON P7B 5L4

Indoor Entertainment for Adults: For families with adult members, OLG Casino Thunder Bay offers indoor entertainment. While not suitable for minors, it provides a rainy-day option for adult family members seeking a bit of excitement.

Rainy days in Thunder Bay become opportunities for family bonding and learning. Rain or shine, Thunder Bay's indoor attractions promise fun and education for the whole family.

Chapter 3

Romantic Escapes

Scenic Walks & Couples' Cruises

Embark on a journey of romance in Thunder Bay, where love intertwines with the stunning natural landscapes and the gentle lull of Lake Superior. Here, you'll discover how to infuse your romantic escapade with the charm of scenic walks and the allure of couples' cruises. Let the untamed north become the backdrop for unforgettable moments shared with your special someone.

Scenic Strolls Hand in Hand

As you set out on your romantic escape, lace up your walking shoes and explore Thunder Bay's picturesque trails. The city offers a myriad of scenic walks, each one presenting an opportunity to connect and create memories.

Marina Park Promenade

Begin your romantic journey at Marina Park, where the serene shores of Lake Superior create a tranquil atmosphere. The Marina Park Promenade invites you to stroll hand in hand along the waterfront, with panoramic views of the lake and the iconic Sleeping Giant in the distance. As you amble through this charming setting, the sound of gentle waves and the fresh breeze set the stage for an intimate experience.

Centennial Park's Lover's Lane

Dive deeper into romance by exploring Lover's Lane in Centennial Park. This enchanting pathway meanders through lush greenery, offering seclusion and a sense of intimacy. Surrounded by nature's embrace, you'll find secluded benches perfect for pausing to enjoy quiet moments together. The rustle of leaves and the occasional song of birds create a natural symphony, adding to the romantic ambiance.

Vickers Park Rose Garden

For a touch of floral romance, make your way to Vickers Park Rose Garden. This hidden gem features beautifully landscaped gardens with a diverse array of roses. Take a stroll among the vibrant blooms, allowing the colors and fragrances to enhance the romance of your journey. The rose garden provides a serene escape within the city, where love blossoms amidst nature's beauty.

Couples' Cruises on Lake Superior

Elevate your romantic escape by setting sail on the pristine waters of Lake Superior. Couples' cruises offer a unique perspective of Thunder Bay's beauty, creating an enchanting experience that unfolds on the open water.

Sunset Cruise

Embark on a romantic voyage with a sunset cruise on Lake Superior. The warm hues of the setting sun cast a golden glow on the water, creating a breathtaking backdrop for your intimate journey. Cruise alongside the Sleeping Giant as the day transitions to night, and witness the sky painted in hues of orange and pink. The gentle rocking of the boat adds a touch of serenity to your shared moments.

Isle Royale Excursion

For a more extended adventure, consider an excursion to Isle Royale. This captivating island, situated in the northwest of Lake Superior, offers couples a secluded retreat. A cruise to Isle Royale provides not only the allure of pristine landscapes but also the opportunity for private exploration. Discover hidden coves, enjoy a picnic on the shores, and let the tranquility of the island enhance the romantic connection between you and your partner.

Starry Night Cruise

As the sun sets and darkness blankets the sky, indulge in a starry night cruise. Away from the city lights, Lake Superior becomes a canvas adorned with countless stars. Cruise under the celestial canopy, sharing quiet moments of wonder as you gaze at the constellations above. The rhythmic sounds of the water create a soothing backdrop, making this cruise a celestial dance for two.

Thus, in Thunder Bay, your romantic escape is not just a journey; it's a collection of moments that form the tapestry of your shared history. Let Thunder Bay be the canvas for your love story, painting each page with the hues of nature, the melody of the water, and the shared whispers of romance.

Unique Dining Experiences & Cozy Cafes

Culinary Delights for Two

In Thunder Bay, romance extends beyond breathtaking landscapes to the realm of exquisite dining experiences. This section unveils the city's culinary tapestry, where each bite is a celebration of love. From unique dining establishments to cozy cafes, let your romantic escapade be a feast for the senses.

Unique Dining Experiences

The Kettle

Begin your gastronomic journey at The Kettle, an intimate restaurant known for its cozy ambiance and delectable cuisine.

Nestled in the heart of Thunder Bay, this culinary gem offers a menu crafted with locally sourced ingredients. Reserve a table for two and savor dishes that blend flavors seamlessly, creating a symphony of tastes to complement your romantic evening.

Caribou Restaurant + Wine Bar

Elevate your dining experience at Caribou Restaurant + Wine Bar, a sophisticated establishment that marries gourmet cuisine with a curated selection of wines. The cozy and welcoming atmosphere creates the perfect stage for an unforgettable evening. Indulge in a culinary voyage as you explore the diverse menu, expertly prepared to satisfy discerning palates. The attentive service ensures that your dining experience is nothing short of perfection.

The Foundry

For a blend of modern elegance and rustic charm, The Foundry beckons. This unique dining venue, housed in a historic building, offers an ambiance that perfectly complements Thunder Bay's romantic allure. Enjoy a menu that fuses contemporary culinary techniques with regional flavors, creating a dining experience that is both delightful and unforgettable.

Cozy Cafes for Intimate Conversations

Bean Fiend Café & Sandwich Bar

Dive into the charm of Bean Fiend Café & Sandwich Bar for a cozy coffee date. This eclectic cafe, adorned with local artwork, provides a laid-back atmosphere perfect for intimate conversations. Share a cup of expertly brewed coffee, indulge in freshly baked pastries, and let the aroma of roasted beans enhance your connection.

Sweet Escape Cake Cafe & Bakery

Satiate your sweet cravings at Sweet Escape Cake Cafe & Bakery. This quaint establishment not only offers delightful pastries and cakes but also creates an atmosphere of warmth and comfort. Enjoy a quiet afternoon indulging in decadent desserts while surrounded by the sweet scent of baked goods and the soft hum of conversation.

The Growing Season Juice Collective

For a refreshing rendezvous, head to The Growing Season Juice Collective. This health-conscious cafe embraces a cozy and eco-friendly setting. Sip on revitalizing juices, savor nourishing snacks, and bask in the inviting atmosphere. The Growing Season provides a unique space for couples seeking a healthier yet equally delightful culinary experience.

As you explore Thunder Bay's unique dining and cafe scene, each bite becomes a shared experience, and every sip deepens the connection between you and your partner. Let the city's culinary offerings be an integral part of your romantic escape, creating moments that linger in your memory long after the meal is over. In Thunder Bay, every restaurant, every cafe, and every bite is an opportunity to weave the narrative of your love story.

Relaxing Spa Treatments & Scenic Lookouts

In the realm of romantic escapes, Thunder Bay beckons couples to immerse themselves in tranquility. Here, I unveil the perfect blend of relaxation with spa treatments and breathtaking views from scenic lookouts. Elevate your romantic journey as you rejuvenate your senses and discover the city's most captivating vantage points.

Relaxing Spa Treatments

The Waters Spa

Begin your journey into serenity at The Waters Spa, where pampering meets perfection. Nestled in a tranquil setting, this spa offers a range of treatments designed to revitalize both body and soul. From couples massages to rejuvenating facials, The Waters Spa ensures a sensory experience that transcends the ordinary. Let the soothing ambiance and skilled therapists transport you to a realm of relaxation.

The BodyMind Centre

For a holistic approach to wellness, The BodyMind Centre awaits your visit. This wellness haven provides a sanctuary for couples seeking balance and rejuvenation. Indulge in therapeutic massages, yoga sessions, and mindfulness practices that foster a sense of harmony. The serene atmosphere and skilled practitioners create an oasis for couples to unwind and connect on a deeper level.

Cascades Day Spa

Cascades Day Spa invites you to a haven of tranquility and indulgence. Immerse yourselves in a world of relaxation with their signature spa packages, incorporating massages, facials, and body treatments. The carefully curated spa rituals ensure a blissful escape, allowing you and your partner to unwind amidst the gentle sounds of cascading water and the soothing scents of essential oils.

Scenic Lookouts

Mount McKay

Ascend to new heights of romance at Mount McKay, one of Thunder Bay's iconic lookouts. As you reach the summit, a panoramic view of the city, Lake Superior, and the surrounding landscapes unfolds before you. Whether you visit during the day to witness the vastness of the lake or choose an evening excursion to admire the city lights, Mount McKay provides a breathtaking backdrop for shared moments.

Trowbridge Falls Park

For a more secluded and nature-infused experience, venture to Trowbridge Falls Park. This hidden gem offers scenic lookouts along the cascading waterfalls of the Current River. Find a quiet spot to sit, breathe in the fresh air, and let the mesmerizing flow of water create a tranquil ambiance. Trowbridge Falls Park invites couples to connect with nature while reveling in the beauty of Thunder Bay.

Hillcrest Park

Discover the romantic allure of Hillcrest Park, where manicured gardens and a charming gazebo create an enchanting atmosphere. This scenic lookout provides a perfect setting for a stroll or a quiet afternoon picnic. With views overlooking the city and Lake Superior, Hillcrest Park offers a picturesque backdrop for couples seeking a blend of nature and urban charm.

In Thunder Bay's realm of romantic escapes, spa treatments, and scenic lookouts intertwine to create moments of bliss and serenity. Let the city's tranquil havens and captivating views become the canvas for your shared narrative of relaxation and romance.

Evening Entertainment & Romantic Getaways

As the sun sets over Thunder Bay, the city comes alive with a tapestry of evening entertainment and romantic getaways. This section unveils the enchanting options that await, ensuring your romantic escape continues to captivate the senses well into the night.

Evening Entertainment

Thunder Bay Community Auditorium

Step into a world of cultural delights at the Thunder Bay Community Auditorium. This venue hosts a variety of performances, from live music concerts to theatrical productions. Attend a captivating show hand in hand, surrounded by the richness of the arts. The auditorium's ambiance sets the stage for an evening filled with a shared appreciation for creativity and talent.

Magnus Theatre

For a more intimate theatrical experience, Magnus Theatre offers an enchanting setting. Attend a live play or a captivating performance in this cozy venue. The dimly lit theater creates an atmosphere of intimacy, allowing you and your partner to immerse yourselves in the magic of storytelling under the soft glow of stage lights.

Waterfront Concert Series

If you prefer the outdoor ambiance, the Waterfront Concert Series is a must-attend. Held in Marina Park during the warmer months, this series features live music performances against the backdrop of Lake Superior. Bring a blanket, settle in on the grass, and let the melodies of talented musicians serenade you and your partner as the sun dips below the horizon.

Romantic Getaways

Elsie's Lakefront Cottages

Escape the hustle and bustle with a romantic getaway at Elsie's Lakefront Cottages. Nestled on the shores of Lake Superior, these charming cottages provide a secluded retreat. Enjoy the serenity of the lake, take strolls along the beach, and savor quiet moments on your private deck. Elsie's Lakefront Cottages offer an idyllic setting for couples seeking a romantic escape immersed in nature.

Prince Arthur Waterfront Hotel & Suites

Experience the allure of cityscape romance at the Prince Arthur Waterfront Hotel & Suites. This elegant hotel, situated along the waterfront, combines luxurious accommodations with picturesque views. Enjoy a romantic dinner at the hotel's restaurant, followed by a stroll along the waterfront promenade. The Prince Arthur Waterfront Hotel & Suites creates an enchanting atmosphere for an intimate urban getaway.

Whispering Pines Log Cottages

Find solace in the rustic charm of Whispering Pines Log Cottages. Tucked away in a forested setting, these cozy cottages offer a romantic escape surrounded by nature. Unwind in a private hot tub, bask in the warmth of a fireplace, and let the tranquil ambiance of the log cabins envelop you and your partner. Whispering Pines Log Cottages provide the perfect hideaway for a secluded and romantic retreat.

In the embrace of Thunder Bay's evening entertainment and romantic getaways, every moment is a brushstroke on the canvas of your shared journey. Whether you opt for the cultural allure of auditorium performances or the secluded charm of a lakeside cottage, let the enchantment of the night sky become the backdrop for crafting memories that will linger in your heart. As the city reveals its nocturnal charm, your romantic escape in Thunder Bay unfolds like a dreamy symphony under the stars.

Chapter 4

Solo Travel

Top Tips for Safe & Enjoyable Adventures

Embarking on a solo journey to Thunder Bay opens up a world of discovery and personal growth. As you prepare for this unique adventure, here are indispensable tips to ensure your solo travel is not just safe but also immensely enjoyable. Thunder Bay, in Canada's untamed north, awaits your independent exploration.

Solo-Friendly Accommodation Options

Your choice of accommodation sets the tone for your solo adventure. Opt for accommodations that prioritize safety, comfort, and a welcoming atmosphere. Thunder Bay offers a range of solo-friendly options, from cozy bed and breakfasts to well-reviewed hostels. Consider staying in the city center for convenience, or choose accommodations with local character in neighborhoods like Waterfront or Bay & Algoma.

Navigating the City

Thunder Bay's layout is conducive to solo exploration. The city is known for its friendly locals, making it easy to ask for directions or recommendations. Utilize the local transit system for efficient and affordable travel between attractions. If you prefer a more personal touch, explore the city on foot, taking in the sights at your own pace. Thunder Bay's compact nature ensures that even solo travelers can cover significant ground without feeling overwhelmed.

Blend In with Local Culture

Immerse yourself in Thunder Bay's local culture by blending in with the community. Attend events, visit local markets, and dine at neighborhood eateries. Engaging with locals not only enhances your experience but also provides insights into Thunder Bay's unique way of life. Don't hesitate to strike up conversations – Thunder Bay residents are known for their warmth and friendliness.

Safety Precautions for Solo Adventurers

Prioritize your safety by taking simple yet crucial precautions. Keep your belongings secure, use well-lit paths during the night, and stay informed about the local emergency services. Thunder Bay is generally a safe destination, but awareness is key to ensuring a worry-free solo adventure. Share your itinerary with someone you trust, and keep a copy of important documents, such as your ID and emergency contacts.

Independent Activities & Tours

Thunder Bay caters to solo travelers with a variety of independent activities and tours. Hike the city's scenic trails, explore the waterfront, or join a solo-friendly guided tour to discover the region's hidden gems. Whether you're interested in outdoor adventures, cultural experiences, or historical explorations, Thunder Bay offers solo-friendly activities that cater to diverse interests.

Affordable & Friendly Dining Experiences

Solo dining in Thunder Bay is a delight, with numerous restaurants offering a warm and inviting atmosphere. Explore the local culinary scene, from seafood to indigenous cuisine, and savor the diverse flavors of the region. Choose eateries with communal seating or friendly staff who can provide recommendations, ensuring that your dining experience is not just a meal but a cultural journey.

Connecting with Fellow Travelers

Solo travel doesn't imply solitude. Thunder Bay provides ample opportunities to connect with fellow adventurers. Join group activities, attend local events, or explore shared accommodations to meet like-minded travelers. Making connections enhances your journey and opens the door to shared experiences and newfound friendships.

Exploring Thunder Bay's Nightlife

While Thunder Bay may not have a bustling nightlife scene, it offers a laid-back and welcoming atmosphere for solo travelers. Enjoy live music at local venues, unwind in cozy pubs, or take a stroll along the waterfront at sunset. Thunder Bay's nightlife may be more relaxed, but it provides a perfect setting for solo travelers seeking a peaceful and enjoyable evening.

Embracing the Silence of Winter

If your solo adventure coincides with the winter months, Thunder Bay transforms into a serene winter wonderland. Engage in winter sports like skiing and snowshoeing, experience the thrill of dog sledding, and marvel at the beauty of snow-covered landscapes. Embrace the unique charm of winter in Thunder Bay, where solitude and nature create a magical atmosphere.

As you prepare for your solo adventure in Thunder Bay, remember that the untamed north of Canada is not just a destination; it's a canvas waiting for your exploration. Embrace the freedom, connect with the welcoming community, and savor the unforgettable moments that solo travel brings. Thunder Bay invites you to discover its beauty, engage in exciting activities, and forge memories that are uniquely yours. Your solo journey begins now.

Affordable & Friendly Accommodation Options

Cozy Bed and Breakfasts in Waterfront - $70 to $120 per night

For a charming and intimate stay, consider the cozy bed and breakfasts nestled along Thunder Bay's scenic Waterfront district. These accommodations provide a warm and welcoming atmosphere, offering personalized services that make solo travelers feel right at home. With prices ranging from $70 to $120 per night, these establishments offer budget-friendly options without compromising on comfort.

Hostels with Local Character in Bay & Algoma - $30 to $60 per night

Solo travelers seeking a vibrant and social atmosphere should explore the hostels in the Bay & Algoma neighborhood. These accommodations, priced between $30 and $60 per night, provide a budget-friendly option without sacrificing the unique character of Thunder Bay. Engage with fellow travelers, share stories, and enjoy the local charm of this lively area.

Convenient City Center Hotels - $80 to $150 per night

For those prioritizing convenience, the City Center boasts a selection of hotels catering to solo adventurers. Positioned near key attractions and transportation hubs, these hotels offer accessibility paired with comfort. Prices range from $80 to $150 per night, making them affordable options for solo travelers seeking both convenience and comfort.

Budget-Friendly Motels near Outdoor Attractions - $60 to $100 per night

If you plan to focus your solo adventure on outdoor activities, consider budget-friendly motels situated near Thunder Bay's natural attractions. With prices ranging from $60 to $100 per night, these motels provide economical options without compromising on proximity to outdoor adventures. Ideal for solo travelers eager to explore the untamed beauty of Thunder Bay.

Solo-Friendly Airbnb Experiences - Varied Pricing

For a more personalized touch, explore the range of Airbnb options available throughout Thunder Bay. Solo travelers can choose from private rooms, entire apartments, or unique accommodations hosted by friendly locals. Prices vary based on accommodation type and location, offering flexibility for different budget preferences. Airbnb experiences allow you to immerse yourself in Thunder Bay's community while enjoying the comforts of a home away from home.

Local Inns with Indigenous Charm - $90 to $130 per night

Immerse yourself in Thunder Bay's rich cultural tapestry by opting for local inns with indigenous charm. Located throughout the city, these inns offer a unique blend of cultural experiences and comfortable accommodations. With prices ranging from $90 to $130 per night, solo travelers can enjoy a distinctive stay that reflects the authenticity of Thunder Bay's indigenous heritage.

Waterfront Cabins for a Tranquil Retreat - $100 to $180 per night

For a serene escape, consider waterfront cabins that provide a tranquil setting along the shores of Lake Superior. Offering solitude and breathtaking views, these cabins allow solo travelers to unwind in nature's embrace. Prices range from $100 to $180 per night, providing a worthwhile investment for those seeking a peaceful retreat amid Thunder Bay's natural beauty.

Shared Accommodations for Social Connections - $40 to $80 per night

Solo travelers eager to connect with fellow adventurers can explore shared accommodations, including guesthouses and communal living spaces. Priced between $40 and $80 per night, these options provide a social atmosphere, encouraging interactions with like-minded travelers. Share stories, tips, and experiences with new friends while exploring Thunder Bay's wonders.

Please, note that prices may vary based on factors such as the time of booking, seasonal demand, and specific accommodation amenities. It's advisable to check with individual establishments for the most up-to-date pricing information.

Independent Activities & Solo-Friendly Tours

Solo Hiking Adventures in Sleeping Giant Provincial Park

Embark on solo hiking adventures amidst the breathtaking landscapes of Sleeping Giant Provincial Park. Trails cater to various skill levels, allowing you to choose your preferred difficulty. Whether conquering the challenging Top of the Giant trail or opting for a stroll along the Sea Lion's Rock path, solo exploration of this park unveils awe-inspiring views of Lake Superior.

Scenic Bike Paths for Solo Cyclists

Thunder Bay boasts scenic bike paths perfect for solo cyclists. Navigate the waterfront trails or venture into the city's neighborhoods on two wheels. Rent a bike from local shops, and pedal your way through picturesque routes like the Trowbridge Falls Loop or the Kaministiquia River Heritage Ride.

Kayaking Adventures on Lake Superior

Solo travelers seeking aquatic thrills can embark on solo kayaking adventures on the vast expanse of Lake Superior. Local outfitters offer kayak rentals and guided tours suitable for individuals. Paddle along the stunning shoreline, explore sea caves, and witness the beauty of Thunder Bay from a unique perspective.

Cultural Exploration at Thunder Bay Art Galleries

Immerse yourself in Thunder Bay's cultural scene with a solo visit to its art galleries. Explore the Thunder Bay Art Gallery, showcasing Indigenous art and contemporary exhibitions. Solo travelers can leisurely appreciate the diverse artistic expressions that contribute to the city's vibrant cultural tapestry.

Historical Journey at Fort William Historical Park

For a solo historical journey, visit Fort William Historical Park. Explore the reconstructed fur trading post and step back in time to the era of the fur trade. Engage in self-guided tours, discovering the historical significance of this site and gaining insights into Thunder Bay's past.

Solo-Friendly Amethyst Mining at Blue Point Amethyst Mine

Venture into the depths of Thunder Bay's geological wonders with a solo-friendly amethyst mining experience at Blue Point Amethyst Mine. Dig for your sparkling treasures or browse the mine shop for unique souvenirs. This off-the-beaten-path activity allows solo travelers to connect with Thunder Bay's rich geological history.

Guided Solo Winter Activities with Dog Sledding Tours

Embrace the winter wonderland of Thunder Bay with solo-friendly dog sledding tours. Local operators offer guided experiences, allowing you to navigate snowy trails while being led by a team of energetic huskies. Discover the tranquility of winter landscapes and the thrill of mushing through the snow-covered wilderness.

Hidden Local Haunts & Unexpected Delights

Solo adventurers can uncover Thunder Bay's hidden gems by exploring local haunts and unexpected delights. Wander through the city's neighborhoods, stumble upon charming cafes, and quirky boutiques, and connect with the authentic character of Thunder Bay. Solo exploration often leads to serendipitous discoveries that enhance the overall travel experience.

Independent Exploration of Public Art Installations

Thunder Bay's streets are adorned with public art installations waiting to be discovered. Take a self-guided tour of the city's murals, sculptures, and outdoor art displays. Navigate the Waterfront Public Art Walk or explore the downtown area to appreciate the diverse artistic expressions that contribute to Thunder Bay's cultural vibrancy.

Solo Adventure Planning at Visitor Information Centers

For personalized solo adventure planning, visit Thunder Bay's Visitor Information Centers. Gather maps, brochures, and recommendations tailored to your interests. Knowledgeable staff can provide insights into solo-friendly activities, ensuring that your independent exploration aligns with your preferences.

Thunder Bay invites solo travelers to tailor their adventure, offering a diverse range of independent activities and solo-friendly tours. Whether you seek outdoor thrills, cultural immersion, or historical exploration, Thunder Bay provides the perfect canvas for solo adventurers to create their unique journeys.

Finding Community & Making Memories

Forge connections and create lasting memories by participating in Thunder Bay's vibrant local events and festivals. Solo travelers can find a sense of community at gatherings like the Live on the Waterfront concert series, the Thunder Bay Blues Festival, or the Kaministiquia River Heritage Festival. Engage with locals, savor live performances, and immerse yourself in the cultural tapestry of Thunder Bay.

Connecting Through Outdoor Group Activities

For solo travelers seeking companionship in outdoor adventures, join group activities organized by local clubs or outdoor enthusiasts. Hiking groups, cycling clubs, and kayaking meetups provide opportunities to connect with like-minded individuals.

Share experiences, swap travel stories, and create bonds over a shared love for adventure.

Attend Indigenous Cultural Events

Immerse yourself in Thunder Bay's Indigenous culture by attending cultural events and gatherings. Look out for powwows, art exhibitions, and traditional ceremonies that offer a glimpse into the rich heritage of the region. Participating in these events not only connects you with the community but also provides a deeper understanding of Thunder Bay's cultural identity.

Engaging in Community Volunteer Opportunities

Contribute to the community and make meaningful connections by engaging in volunteer opportunities. Thunder Bay hosts various community initiatives, environmental projects, and charitable events. Joining a volunteer program not only allows you to give back but also introduces you to locals who share a passion for making a positive impact.

Exploring Shared Accommodations and Communal Spaces

Opt for shared accommodations or communal spaces that foster social interactions. Hostels, guesthouses, and co-living spaces create environments where solo travelers can connect with others. Share a meal in a communal kitchen, participate in organized activities, and build camaraderie with fellow adventurers staying in the same accommodation.

Participate in Local Workshops and Classes

Enrich your solo journey by participating in local workshops and classes. Whether it's a cooking class, an art workshop, or a fitness session, these activities provide opportunities to meet locals with shared interests. Attend classes at community centers, studios, or cultural institutions to both learn new skills and make connections.

Socialize in Laid-Back Cafés and Waterfront Hangouts

Thunder Bay's laid-back cafés and waterfront hangouts are perfect settings for solo travelers to socialize. Strike up conversations with locals at coffee shops like Bean Fiend or enjoy the scenic views while chatting with fellow visitors at Prince Arthur's Landing. The relaxed atmosphere encourages interactions, making it easy to find community in unexpected places.

Engage with Locals at Farmers' Markets

Explore Thunder Bay's farmers' markets, such as the Thunder Bay Country Market or the Waterfront Artisan Market. Engaging with local vendors and shoppers provides an authentic glimpse into the community's daily life. Sample local delicacies, discover handmade crafts, and strike up conversations with friendly locals.

Attend Language Exchange Meetups

For language enthusiasts, attend language exchange meetups where locals and travelers gather to practice different languages. Thunder Bay's language exchange events provide an informal setting to meet new people, exchange cultural insights, and build connections through shared linguistic interests.

Utilize Social Media and Travel Forums

In the digital age, social media and travel forums offer platforms to connect with other solo travelers and locals. Join Thunder Bay-specific groups, forums, or online communities to seek advice, share experiences, and possibly arrange meetups with fellow adventurers. Virtual connections can often transition into real-life friendships.

In Thunder Bay, finding community as a solo traveler goes beyond shared activities; it's about connecting with the heart and soul of the city. Whether you're dancing at a festival, exploring Indigenous culture, or sharing stories in a waterfront café, Thunder Bay invites you to create memories and build relationships that will last a lifetime. Your solo journey transforms into a shared array of experiences, woven together with the vibrant threads of Thunder Bay's welcoming community.

Part 2

Discovering Thunder Bay's Treasures

Chapter 5

Geography & Climate

Lake Superior's Majestic Presence

Begin your exploration of Thunder Bay by immersing yourself in the awe-inspiring presence of Lake Superior. Stretching endlessly before you, this immense freshwater giant holds the title of the world's largest freshwater lake by surface area. The sheer magnitude of Lake Superior, visible from various points in Thunder Bay, sets the stage for an extraordinary journey into the heart of natural wonder.

A Glimpse of Superior's Grandeur

Standing on the shores of Thunder Bay, you witness the vastness of Lake Superior, a sight that leaves an indelible mark on your senses. The expansive horizon, uninterrupted by land on the opposite shore, gives you a profound sense of the lake's sheer enormity. The waters, ranging from deep blues to emerald greens, mirror the ever-changing moods of the sky above, creating a living canvas that unfolds before your eyes.

Exploring the Coastal Beauty

Venture along Thunder Bay's coastline, where Lake Superior reveals its diverse personalities. Serene bays invite you to stroll along sandy shores, while rugged cliffs and rocky outcrops provide vantage points for absorbing panoramic views. Engage in lakeside activities such as kayaking or paddleboarding, allowing you to become one with the tranquil waters of Superior. The pristine beauty of the lake's shoreline sets the scene for moments of contemplation and connection with nature.

Seasonal Transitions of Lake Superior

Lake Superior is not static; it's a dynamic entity that undergoes remarkable transformations with the changing seasons. In the warmer months, feel the gentle caress of the lake breeze as you indulge in water activities or simply relax on the shores. As autumn arrives, witness the dance of colors as the foliage surrounding the lake transforms into a breathtaking tapestry of reds, yellows, and oranges. Winter casts a serene spell over the lake, transforming it into a frozen expanse that invites winter enthusiasts to explore its icy wonders.

Understanding the Power of the Lake

Lake Superior's majesty is not only visual; it resonates in the power of its waves and the whispers of its winds. Feel the force of the lake as waves crash against the rocky shores, a reminder of the untamed nature of this northern gem. Be cautious and respect the lake's power, especially during stormy weather, as Lake Superior demands both admiration and reverence.

Adapting to Thunder Bay's Diverse Climate

Lake Superior significantly influences Thunder Bay's climate, contributing to a unique weather pattern that varies throughout the year. Embrace the crispness of the air during winter, where snow blankets the landscape, and frozen surfaces invite winter sports enthusiasts to partake in the seasonal delights. In the warmer months, bask in the gentle warmth of the sun as you explore outdoor trails and engage in water-based activities.

Dressing for the Elements

Pack accordingly as you prepare to face Thunder Bay's diverse climate. In winter, ensure you're equipped with insulated layers, waterproof gear, and sturdy boots to navigate the snowy terrain comfortably. During the milder seasons, opt for breathable clothing suitable for outdoor adventures, and always have a light jacket on hand, as the weather around Lake Superior can be unpredictable.

Geography Unveiled

Lake Superior is not just a scenic backdrop but an integral part of Thunder Bay's geographical tapestry. Its influence extends beyond visual aesthetics, shaping the city's culture, history, and recreational opportunities. As you stand before the majesty of Lake Superior, you are not merely a spectator; you are a participant in the rhythmic dance between land and water, a dance that defines the essence of Thunder Bay. The geography of this region, intricately tied to the lake's presence, becomes a map guiding you through an exploration of natural wonders and cultural treasures.

Landscapes & Ecosystems

As you traverse Thunder Bay's expansive terrain, you'll encounter diverse landscapes that showcase the region's natural richness.

Boreal Forests

Explore the vast boreal forests that blanket Thunder Bay's hinterland. These expansive woodlands, dominated by coniferous trees such as spruce and pine, create a lush tapestry of greenery. Head to Sleeping Giant Provincial Park to witness the boreal forests at their most pristine, offering a haven for hikers and nature enthusiasts. The scent of pine fills the air as you navigate the trails, providing an immersive experience in the heart of Canada's wilderness.

Rugged Cliffs and Shorelines

Thunder Bay's northern charm extends to its rugged cliffs and rocky shorelines, especially along the shores of Lake Superior. Kakabeka Falls, often referred to as the "Niagara of the North," is surrounded by these dramatic cliffs, showcasing the power of water against ancient rock formations. Feel the mist on your face as you stand in awe of this natural wonder, appreciating the resilience of the landscape shaped by centuries of geological processes.

Old-Growth Forests

Immerse yourself in the timeless beauty of Thunder Bay's old-growth forests, where ancient trees stand as sentinels of the region's ecological history. The Nipigon River Recreation Trail takes you through portions of these majestic forests, offering a glimpse into ecosystems that have evolved over centuries. Towering trees, some reaching ages over 300 years, create a cathedral-like ambiance, providing a sacred space for reflection and appreciation of nature's resilience.

Coastal Sand Dunes

Venture towards the coastal areas, where pristine sand dunes adorn the shores of Lake Superior. These coastal sand dunes, found in pockets along the lake's edge, contribute to Thunder Bay's ecological diversity. Traverse the trails near Chippewa Park, where the juxtaposition of sandy expanses against the backdrop of the lake presents a unique ecosystem that supports specialized plant life and provides a habitat for coastal birds.

Limestone Karst Formations

Uncover Thunder Bay's geological wonders in the form of limestone karst formations. The Shebandowan Lakes Karst Reserve showcases these unique landscapes, characterized by sinkholes, caves, and underground streams. Embark on guided tours to explore this subterranean world, marveling at the intricate formations sculpted by the forces of nature over millennia.

Expansive Meadows

In contrast to the dense forests and rocky shores, Thunder Bay boasts expansive meadows that come alive with vibrant wildflowers during the warmer months. These picturesque meadows, scattered throughout the region, offer serene spots for picnics or moments of quiet contemplation. Pay a visit to Centennial Botanical Conservatory, where carefully curated gardens showcase the diversity of plant life in Thunder Bay's meadows.

Ecosystems Teeming with Life

The landscapes of Thunder Bay host a rich array of ecosystems, each contributing to the area's biodiversity.

Aquatic Ecosystems

Lake Superior, with its crystal-clear waters, is the primary source of aquatic life in Thunder Bay. Dive into the underwater world of the lake, teeming with species like lake trout, whitefish, and sturgeon. The aquatic ecosystems extend to the numerous inland lakes surrounding Thunder Bay, offering opportunities for freshwater fishing and exploration.

Wetlands and Marshes

Venture into Thunder Bay's wetlands and marshes, essential ecosystems that support diverse flora and fauna. These areas, such as the Mission Marsh Conservation Area, provide crucial habitats for migratory birds and amphibians. Birdwatchers will delight in the opportunity to spot a variety of waterfowl and songbirds amidst the lush greenery.

Alpine Ecosystems

Ascend to higher elevations, and you'll encounter alpine ecosystems characterized by unique plant life adapted to colder and harsher conditions. The elevated regions of Sleeping Giant Provincial Park showcase alpine flora, offering a stark yet beautiful contrast to the landscapes found at lower altitudes.

Hidden Valleys and Breathtaking Vistas

Thunder Bay unveils hidden valleys and breathtaking vistas, adding layers to its diverse landscapes.

Valleys and Gorges

Delve into Thunder Bay's hidden valleys and gorges, where meandering rivers carve through the landscape, creating pockets of verdant beauty. Explore the Kaministiquia River Valley, a haven for hikers and nature lovers. Traverse scenic trails that wind along the riverbanks, providing glimpses of waterfalls and panoramic views of the surrounding valleys. The synergy of flowing water and lush greenery creates a serene escape within Thunder Bay's topographical tapestry.

Elevated Plateaus

Discover elevated plateaus that offer expansive views of the surrounding landscapes. The Nor'Wester Mountains, located just west of Thunder Bay, provide an elevated vantage point to behold the city, Lake Superior, and beyond. Hike or drive to these elevated plateaus for breathtaking sunsets that paint the skies in hues of pink and orange, casting a warm glow over Thunder Bay's diverse terrains.

Preserving the Fragile Balance

Thunder Bay recognizes the delicate balance of its ecosystems and endeavors to preserve these natural treasures. Conservation initiatives and designated protected areas underscore the city's commitment to ensuring the longevity of its diverse landscapes and ecosystems. As you tread lightly through these hidden valleys, elevated plateaus, old-growth forests, and unique coastal features, you become a guardian of Thunder Bay's ecological tapestry, contributing to the ongoing narrative of environmental stewardship in Canada's untamed north.

Understanding the Seasons & Weather Patterns

Thunder Bay dances to the rhythm of distinct seasons, each contributing to the city's charm and offering a unique canvas for exploration.

Vibrant Spring

As the grip of winter loosens, Thunder Bay awakens in a burst of color and vitality. Spring brings a gradual thaw, with buds transforming into blossoms, carpeting the city in hues of pink, white, and lavender. Embrace the rejuvenating energy of spring as you stroll through parks and gardens, witnessing the emergence of life after the winter slumber. Pleasant temperatures make it an ideal season for hiking trails that come alive with the sounds of birds and rustling leaves.

Sunlit Summer

Experience the sunlit embrace of Thunder Bay's summer, where the days stretch long, inviting you to indulge in outdoor adventures. Warm temperatures create the perfect setting for kayaking on Lake Superior, exploring biking trails, and basking in the sun on sandy shores. Summer nights bring a gentle coolness, allowing for strolls along the waterfront or vibrant nights out in the city. Festivals and outdoor events dot the calendar, adding a lively backdrop to your summer escapades.

Colorful Autumn

As summer bids adieu, Thunder Bay transforms into a canvas of reds, oranges, and golds. Autumn paints the landscapes in a breathtaking tapestry of colors, inviting you to witness the changing foliage. The crisp air carries the scent of fallen leaves as you explore trails surrounded by a kaleidoscope of autumn hues. Fall is an opportune time for scenic drives, capturing the picturesque landscapes, and visiting orchards offering seasonal delights.

Winter Wonderland

When winter descends upon Thunder Bay, the city transforms into a magical wonderland blanketed in snow. Winter enthusiasts can revel in a plethora of activities, from cross-country skiing through snowy trails to ice fishing on frozen lakes. The festive atmosphere is heightened by winter events and the possibility of witnessing the mesmerizing aurora borealis. Bundle up and embrace the winter charm, where the world becomes hushed under a blanket of snow, creating a serene backdrop for winter adventures.

Weather Patterns

Understanding Thunder Bay's weather patterns is essential for planning a seamless exploration throughout the seasons.

Lake Influence

Lake Superior plays a pivotal role in shaping Thunder Bay's weather. The lake's moderating effect ensures milder temperatures along the shores, influencing the city's climate. During winter, the lake can mitigate extreme cold temperatures, while in summer, it provides a refreshing breeze.

Snowfall in Winter

Winter brings generous snowfall to Thunder Bay, transforming the landscape into a snowy wonderland. The abundance of snow opens doors to a host of winter activities, including snowshoeing, skiing, and snowmobiling. Be prepared for snowy adventures and relish the unique charm of Thunder Bay's winter offerings.

Autumn Showers

Autumn may bring occasional rainfall, enhancing the vibrancy of fall foliage. While the showers are typically moderate, it's advisable to carry appropriate gear if you plan on exploring outdoor attractions during this season.

Summer Warmth

Summer in Thunder Bay is characterized by warm temperatures, providing an inviting environment for outdoor pursuits. Pack lightweight clothing, and sunscreen, and stay hydrated as you engage in activities under the sunny skies.

Whether you're drawn to the blossoming beauty of spring, the sunlit warmth of summer, the vibrant colors of autumn, or the enchanting winter landscapes, Thunder Bay invites you to tailor your visit according to the changing seasons. Understanding the ebb and flow of weather patterns ensures that your exploration aligns harmoniously with the city's seasonal symphony. So, pack accordingly, and let each season unfold a new chapter in your Thunder Bay adventure.

Dressing for the Diverse Climate

Thunder Bay's diverse climate requires a thoughtful approach to dressing, ensuring your comfort and enjoyment throughout the changing seasons.

Winter Essentials

Winters in Thunder Bay are synonymous with a magical snowy landscape, making proper attire essential for cold-weather exploration. Equip yourself with insulated layers, including a waterproof and windproof outer shell. Thermal undergarments, a sturdy pair of insulated boots, and warm gloves are crucial for outdoor activities like snowshoeing, skiing, or simply enjoying a walk in the winter wonderland. A cozy hat and a scarf to protect against chilly winds complete your winter ensemble.

Spring Layers

As spring unfolds, temperatures vary, requiring a versatile wardrobe. Layering is key during this transitional season. A light waterproof jacket is handy for spring showers, while breathable layers underneath allow you to adapt to changing temperatures. Comfortable hiking boots and waterproof footwear are essential for exploring muddy trails and wet terrain. Don't forget sunglasses and sunscreen as the sun gains strength during spring.

Summer Comfort

Summers in Thunder Bay bring warmth and a plethora of outdoor activities. Pack lightweight, breathable clothing to stay cool during sunny days. Sunscreen, a wide-brimmed hat, and sunglasses are essential for sun protection. If you plan to engage in water activities on Lake Superior, bring swimwear, a beach towel, and water-resistant sandals. Comfortable walking shoes are ideal for exploring parks and trails.

Fall Ready Attire

Fall's crisp air and changing foliage necessitate clothing that provides warmth without being too bulky. Bring a mix of long-sleeved shirts, sweaters, and a light jacket for layering. Comfortable hiking boots are suitable for exploring trails adorned with autumn colors. As temperatures drop in the evening, having a warm hat and gloves is advisable.

All-Season Essentials

Certain items are useful year-round in Thunder Bay. A durable and waterproof backpack ensures your belongings stay dry during unexpected rain or snow. A water bottle keeps you hydrated during hikes, while a compact umbrella offers protection from rain showers. Regardless of the season, insect repellent can be essential, especially during outdoor activities in wooded areas.

Local Fashion Tips

Thunder Bay locals embrace a casual and functional approach to fashion. Comfortable and weather-appropriate clothing is favored, reflecting the city's outdoor lifestyle. Don't forget to include a pair of good walking shoes, suitable for exploring the diverse terrains that Thunder Bay has to offer.

Additional Considerations

Always check the weather forecast before embarking on outdoor adventures, as conditions can change rapidly. Thunder Bay's weather can be unpredictable, so having a light rain jacket or an extra layer in your bag is a practical precaution. Be mindful of the specific activities you plan to engage in and adjust your wardrobe accordingly to make the most of your Thunder Bay experience.

By adapting your wardrobe to Thunder Bay's diverse climate, you ensure a comfortable and enjoyable exploration of the city's natural wonders throughout the seasons. Whether you're gazing at frozen waterfalls in winter or hiking through colorful landscapes in fall, the right clothing enhances your experience, allowing you to fully embrace the beauty of Canada's untamed north.

Chapter 6

History & Culture

In your journey through Thunder Bay, the thread of indigenous heritage and traditions weaves seamlessly into the vibrant tapestry of the region. Let's delve into the rich history that shaped the culture of Thunder Bay and explore the unique traditions that continue to flourish.

Indigenous Heritage & Traditions

Connecting with the Anishinaabe People

As you step into Thunder Bay, you step onto the ancestral lands of the Anishinaabe people. This Indigenous community, rooted deeply in Thunder Bay's history, contributes significantly to the cultural identity of the region. Encounter the Anishinaabe language, Ojibwe, spoken and celebrated, offering you a glimpse into a language that echoes through generations.

Sacred Sites and Spiritual Practices

Explore the sacred sites that hold profound significance for the Anishinaabe people. Witness the majestic energy at Mount McKay, known as Animikii-wajiw (Thunderbird Mountain), a sacred place where spiritual practices are performed. The mesmerizing vistas from this sacred site provide not only panoramic views of Thunder Bay but also a connection to the spiritual realm embraced by the Anishinaabe.

Drum Circles and Powwows

Engage in the heartbeat of Anishinaabe culture through drum circles and powwows. These rhythmic gatherings are not merely performances; they are expressions of community, tradition, and spirituality. The steady beat of the drums reverberates through the air, inviting you to join the dance and feel the unity that comes from participating in age-old traditions.

Traditional Arts and Crafts

Immerse yourself in the world of traditional arts and crafts, where skilled artisans share their heritage through intricate beadwork, quillwork, and basketry. Visit local markets and galleries to witness the beauty of handmade crafts, each piece carrying the essence of Anishinaabe identity and storytelling.

Smudging Ceremonies

Participate in smudging ceremonies, a sacred ritual involving the burning of medicinal herbs like sweetgrass, sage, and cedar. This purification process is a deeply spiritual practice, cleansing the mind, body, and spirit. Engage respectfully, guided by the wisdom of the Anishinaabe people, and embrace the transformative power of this age-old ceremony.

Culinary Traditions

Savor the flavors of indigenous cuisine, where traditional ingredients and preparation methods reflect a deep connection to the land. Indigenous culinary traditions often include wild game, freshwater fish, and foraged plants, providing a taste of the rich biodiversity that Thunder Bay offers. Allow your taste buds to journey through the cultural tapestry woven into each dish.

Interacting with Elders

Respectfully engage with the elders of the Anishinaabe community. These revered individuals carry the wisdom of generations, serving as storytellers and guardians of tradition. Attend community events or seek out cultural centers to participate in conversations that offer insights into the enduring legacy of the Anishinaabe people.

Community Events and Celebrations

Stay attuned to community events and celebrations that showcase the liveliness of indigenous culture. From the Annual Anishinaabe Arts Festival to cultural gatherings, these events offer a dynamic experience where you can witness traditional dances, storytelling, and contemporary expressions of Anishinaabe identity.

Preserving and Honoring Indigenous Heritage

Recognize the ongoing efforts to preserve and honor indigenous heritage in Thunder Bay. Support local initiatives that focus on cultural revitalization, language preservation, and community empowerment. By understanding and respecting the ongoing journey of the Anishinaabe people, you contribute to the preservation of Thunder Bay's rich cultural tapestry.

As you navigate the intricate chapters of Thunder Bay's indigenous heritage, remember that each experience is an opportunity to appreciate the resilience, wisdom, and beauty embedded in the traditions of the Anishinaabe people. Your journey becomes a celebration of cultural diversity and a profound connection to the living history of Thunder Bay.

Fur Trade Legacy & Fort William Historical Park

As you stand on the shores of Thunder Bay, imagine the bustling activity of the fur trade era that once defined this region. The fur trade, a cornerstone of Canada's economic history, shaped the destinies of nations and cultures. Thunder Bay, strategically located at the crossroads of waterways, became a pivotal hub for fur trading posts.

Fort William Historical Park: A Living Chronicle

Your journey through Thunder Bay's fur trade legacy culminates at Fort William Historical Park, an open-air living museum that transports you back to the early 19th century. Fort William, a prominent North West Company trading post, reconstructed meticulously, offers an immersive experience where history comes to life.

Trading Post Dynamics

Step into the shoes of fur traders as you explore the reconstructed trading post. Witness the lively exchange of goods, the negotiation of fur bales, and the diverse array of cultures converging at this economic epicenter. Engage with costumed interpreters who breathe life into historical characters, providing insights into the complexities of the fur trade.

Voyageur Lifestyle

Envision yourself as a voyageur, part of the intrepid workforce that paddled vast waterways, braving the challenges of the Canadian wilderness. At Fort William Historical Park, participate in hands-on experiences that capture the essence of a voyageur's daily life –

from canoeing to crafting, immerse yourself in the skills required for survival.

Cultural Fusion at Fort William

As you explore the fort's grounds, observe the harmonious cultural fusion that characterized life during the fur trade era. Indigenous peoples, European traders, and Métis inhabitants coexisted, forging connections that transcended cultural boundaries. Engage in conversations with historical reenactors to gain a deeper understanding of this unique period of cultural exchange.

Events and Festivals

Time your visit to coincide with events and festivals that breathe vitality into Fort William Historical Park. The Rendezvous, a lively gathering of historical enthusiasts, showcases period-specific competitions, demonstrations, and festivities. The energy of these events transports you back to an era where fur traders and Indigenous communities converged in celebration.

Fur Trade Challenges and Triumphs

Delve into the challenges faced by fur traders – from the harsh wilderness conditions to the intricacies of trade negotiations. Gain an appreciation for the resilience and adaptability required to navigate the unpredictable landscape of the fur trade. The interactive exhibits and guided tours at Fort William Historical Park provide a nuanced perspective on the triumphs and tribulations of this pivotal era.

Educational Programs for All Ages

Fort William Historical Park offers educational programs catering to all ages, making it an enriching experience for families, history enthusiasts, and students alike. Engage in workshops, demonstrations, and guided tours that offer a comprehensive insight into the fur trade legacy and its lasting impact on the Thunder Bay region.

Preservation Efforts and Legacy Building

Acknowledge the ongoing preservation efforts at Fort William Historical Park, ensuring that the legacy of the fur trade era remains accessible to future generations. Support the initiatives aimed at maintaining the authenticity of the site and fostering an understanding of Thunder Bay's integral role in shaping Canada's economic and cultural tapestry.

As you journey through the fur trade legacy and Fort William Historical Park, each step unveils a chapter of history that is both immersive and enlightening. Your time at Fort William becomes more than a visit; it becomes a profound connection to the resilience, ingenuity, and enduring spirit of those who shaped Thunder Bay's past.

Arts & Culture Scene: Galleries, Museums & Festivals

In your exploration of Thunder Bay's rich history and culture, the chapter on the arts and culture scene becomes a colorful tapestry that unfolds as a testament to the city's creative spirit. Journey through the dynamic expressions of Thunder Bay's artistic landscape, from captivating galleries to enlightening museums and lively festivals.

Galleries: A Canvas of Creativity

Thunder Bay Art Gallery

Located at 1080 Keewatin Street, the Thunder Bay Art Gallery stands as a beacon of artistic expression. Immerse yourself in a diverse collection of contemporary and Indigenous art. The gallery's commitment to showcasing regional and national artists ensures a rich and varied experience. Keep an eye on their rotating exhibitions and special events for a dynamic exploration of visual arts.

Definitely Superior Art Gallery

Nestled in the heart of Thunder Bay's downtown at 250 Park Avenue, the Definitely Superior Art Gallery is a hub for avant-garde and experimental art. Explore the edgy and thought-provoking exhibits that challenge conventions. The gallery's commitment to fostering emerging artists and pushing the boundaries of creativity adds a unique dimension to Thunder Bay's art scene.

Museums: Unveiling the Past

Thunder Bay Museum

Embark on a historical journey at the Thunder Bay Museum, located at 425 Donald Street East. Explore exhibits that chronicle the city's evolution from its Indigenous roots to the bustling metropolis it is today. The museum's focus on local history provides an insightful narrative, offering a comprehensive understanding of Thunder Bay's heritage.

Founders' Museum & Pioneer Village

Travel back in time at the Founders' Museum & Pioneer Village, situated at 3300 Highway 61. This living history museum recreates Thunder Bay's early settlement, complete with period buildings and artifacts. Engage with costumed interpreters who transport you to the pioneering days, providing an authentic experience of Thunder Bay's foundational years.

Festivals: Celebrate the Cultural Rhythm

The Bay & Algoma Buskers Festival

Join the lively festivities of The Bay & Algoma Buskers Festival, an annual celebration of street performance and artistic talent. Wander through the vibrant Bay & Algoma neighborhood during mid-July, where musicians, jugglers, and entertainers fill the streets, creating an atmosphere of joy and spontaneity.

Live on the Waterfront

Experience Thunder Bay's music scene comes alive at Live on the Waterfront, a summer concert series held at Marina Park (1 Cumberland St N). Every Wednesday evening from mid-July to late August, revel in diverse musical genres performed against the picturesque backdrop of Lake Superior. It's a harmonious blend of culture, community, and natural beauty.

Die Active Art Collective's Nuit Blanche

Witness the city transform during Die Active Art Collective's Nuit Blanche, an all-night contemporary art festival. Taking place in the downtown area around September, Nuit Blanche features interactive installations, performances, and exhibitions, turning Thunder Bay into a nocturnal canvas of creativity and expression.

Bay Street Film Festival

Celebrate the art of cinema at the Bay Street Film Festival, an annual event that showcases independent and international films. Held in early September at various locations, this festival provides a platform for filmmakers to share diverse narratives. Engage in thought-provoking discussions and immerse yourself in the cinematic arts during this cultural highlight.

Harvest Festival

Savor the flavors of Thunder Bay's cultural diversity at the Harvest Festival, typically held in late September at Marina Park. This culinary celebration brings together local chefs, artisans, and musicians, offering a sensory journey through the region's culinary arts. Engage in food tastings, workshops, and live performances during this vibrant festival.

As you navigate Thunder Bay's arts and culture scene, each gallery, museum, and festival becomes a brushstroke in the city's cultural canvas. Whether you're delving into the visual arts, exploring the city's history, or reveling in the rhythm of festivals, Thunder Bay invites you to partake in its vibrant and ever-evolving cultural narrative.

Local Flavors & Culinary Delights

Dishes That Define Thunder Bay's Culinary Landscape

Persian Manoosh

Treat your taste buds to the unique flavor of Thunder Bay's iconic Persian Manoosh. Head to The Persian Manoosh Bakery on 40 Cumberland Street South to indulge in this local delight. A delectable combination of sweet dough, cinnamon, and butter, this treat has become a cultural symbol of Thunder Bay. Cost: $2.50 per piece.

Walleye

Experience the freshness of Lake Superior with a plate of walleye, a local favorite. Enjoy this flaky whitefish prepared with culinary expertise at restaurants like Bight Restaurant & Bar (2200 Sleeping Giant Pkwy). The cost for a walleye dish typically ranges from $20 to $30, depending on the presentation and accompanying sides.

Caribou

For a unique culinary experience, savor the flavors of caribou at restaurants like Caribou Restaurant + Wine Bar (727 Hewitson Street). This exotic meat is prepared with local flair, offering a taste of Thunder Bay's northern influence. A caribou dish may cost around $35 to $45, reflecting the premium quality and rarity of the meat.

Tourtière Poutine

Indulge in a Canadian classic with a Thunder Bay twist – Tourtière Poutine. Head to The Sovereign Room at 220 Red River Road for this creative fusion. Enjoy the traditional Quebecois meat pie flavors atop a bed of crispy fries, smothered in savory gravy and cheese curds. The cost for this indulgent dish is around $15.

Pickerel Cheeks

Delight in the delicate flavors of pickerel cheeks, a seafood delicacy often featured on the menu at restaurants like Tomlin Restaurant (202 Syndicate Avenue South). Prepared with precision and served with complementary sides, a plate of pickerel cheeks may cost between $25 and $35.

Bison Burger

Satisfy your burger cravings with a Thunder Bay twist – the Bison Burger. Make your way to Nook Thunder Bay (499 Ray Blvd) for this hearty and flavorful dish. The cost for a bison burger, accompanied by fresh toppings and artisanal buns, is typically around $18.

Local Craft Brews

Pair your culinary adventures with Thunder Bay's thriving craft beer scene. Explore local breweries like Sleeping Giant Brewing Co. and Dawson Trail Craft Brewery, where a pint of craft beer can range from $6 to $8. Indulge in unique brews that capture the essence of Thunder Bay's rugged landscapes.

Perch Tacos

Head to the Hoito Restaurant (314 Bay Street) and savor the flavors of Thunder Bay with Perch Tacos. This local favorite combines fresh perch, crisp veggies, and zesty toppings. The cost for a plate of perch tacos typically ranges from $15 to $20.

Wild Blueberry Pie

Conclude your culinary journey with a slice of Thunder Bay's Wild Blueberry Pie. Visit The Sweet North Bakery (1700 King's Highway) for a taste of this regional dessert, where the cost for a slice is approximately $5. Indulge in the sweet and tart flavors of locally sourced wild blueberries.

Venison Sausages with Saskatoon Berry Compote

Dive into the fusion of flavors at Prime Gelato (310 Bay Street) with Venison Sausages paired with Saskatoon Berry Compote. This delightful dish combines the richness of venison sausages with the sweet-tartness of Saskatoon berries. The cost for this unique culinary creation is approximately $22.

Smoked Lake Trout Dip

Experience the smoky goodness of Thunder Bay's Smoked Lake Trout Dip. Head to The Growing Season Juice Collective (268 Red River Road) to savor this appetizing spread. Accompanied by fresh bread or crackers, this local favorite is priced around $12.

Vegan Delights at The Sovereign Room

For plant-based culinary enthusiasts, The Sovereign Room (220 Red River Road) offers a diverse selection of vegan delights. Indulge in dishes like Vegan Nachos or the Quinoa Power Bowl, priced between $15 and $20, showcasing Thunder Bay's commitment to inclusive and delicious dining.

Lakehead Burger

Sink your teeth into the Lakehead Burger at The Foundry (242 Red River Road). This hearty creation features local beef, cheese, and a special sauce, capturing the essence of Thunder Bay's culinary innovation. The cost for this delectable burger is approximately $16.

Whitefish Tacos

Explore the coastal flavors of Lake Superior with Whitefish Tacos at Bight Restaurant & Bar (2200 Sleeping Giant Pkwy). Freshly caught whitefish, paired with vibrant toppings, creates a taco experience priced around $18.

Craft Cocktails at Red Lion Smokehouse

Enhance your dining experience with craft cocktails at Red Lion Smokehouse (28 Cumberland Street South). From innovative concoctions to classic favorites, indulge in a cocktail for approximately $10 to $14, elevating your culinary journey with carefully crafted libations.

Regional Cheese Platter at Tomlin Restaurant

Embark on a cheese-tasting adventure with the Regional Cheese Platter at Tomlin Restaurant (202 Syndicate Avenue South). Featuring a selection of local cheeses, preserves, and artisanal crackers, this exquisite platter is priced at around $20.

Blueberry Bison Sausages

Delight your palate with the unique blend of flavors in Blueberry Bison Sausages, a culinary gem at Nook Thunder Bay (499 Ray Blvd). The sweet notes of blueberries complement the savory bison, creating a dish priced around $22.

Bannock Tacos with Wild Game

Experience Indigenous culinary traditions with Bannock Tacos featuring wild game at The Caribou Restaurant + Wine Bar (727 Hewitson Street). This culturally rich dish is priced around $25, offering a taste of Thunder Bay's historical and gastronomic heritage.

Thunder Bay Craft Pizza at The Growing Season Juice Collective

Savor a slice of Thunder Bay's culinary creativity with the Thunder Bay Craft Pizza at The Growing Season Juice Collective (268 Red River Road). Topped with fresh, locally sourced ingredients, this artisanal pizza is priced at around $16.

As you navigate Thunder Bay's culinary delights, each dish becomes a portal to the city's diverse flavors and cultural influences. Whether you're savoring the sweetness of Persian Manoosh or indulging in the richness of caribou, Thunder Bay's gastronomic scene promises a culinary journey filled with memorable tastes and unique experiences.

Part 3

Unveiling the Untamed North

Chapter 7

Outdoor Adventures

Hiking & Trekking Trails: From Easy to Challenging

Thunder Bay boasts an extensive network of hiking trails, catering to all skill levels and preferences. Whether you seek a stroll amidst nature's beauty or a challenging trek that pushes your limits, Thunder Bay has a trail for you.

Centennial Park Trail: Easy Stroll Amidst Urban Greenery

For a relaxed introduction to Thunder Bay's outdoor charm, the Centennial Park Trail awaits. This easy trail meanders through lush urban greenery, offering a perfect escape for those looking to unwind without venturing too far from the city. Enjoy the tranquility of the park, dotted with vibrant flora and the soothing melody of birdsong.

Sleeping Giant Lookout Trail: Moderate Adventure with Scenic Rewards

For a moderate challenge with breathtaking vistas, the Sleeping Giant Lookout Trail beckons. This trail winds through the rugged beauty of Sleeping Giant Provincial Park, gradually ascending to unveil panoramic views of Lake Superior. As you ascend, the captivating silhouette of the Sleeping Giant formation emerges, creating a backdrop that is both awe-inspiring and Instagram-worthy.

Kabeyun Trail: Challenging Cliffs and Wilderness Immersion

Challenge your adventurous spirit with the Kabeyun Trail, known for its rugged terrain and dramatic cliffs. This trail immerses you in the heart of the wilderness, presenting a series of challenging ascents and descents. The reward? Spectacular views of Lake Superior, the rugged coastline, and an unparalleled sense of accomplishment. Be prepared for a full-day trek that promises both physical exertion and unforgettable moments.

Top of the Giant Trail: Summit Thunder Bay's Iconic Landmark

For the ultimate hiking challenge and an opportunity to conquer Thunder Bay's iconic landmark, the Top of the Giant Trail awaits. As you ascend, you'll navigate steep inclines and rocky terrain, but the payoff is unmatched. Stand atop the Sleeping Giant, surveying the vastness of Lake Superior and the surrounding wilderness. This trail is not for the faint of heart, but the sense of triumph at the summit is a memory you'll carry with you forever.

Trekking Trails

For those seeking a more prolonged and immersive adventure, Thunder Bay offers trekking trails that venture deep into its pristine wilderness.

Casque Isles Trail: Coastal Beauty and Tranquil Shorelines

The Casque Isles Trail promises a trekking experience that unfolds along the Lake Superior coastline. Traverse diverse landscapes, from lush forests to tranquil shorelines. With multiple access points, you can customize your trekking experience, exploring sections that align with your time and energy. The rhythmic sound of waves accompanies you as you trek, creating a soothing backdrop to your journey.

Superior Coastal Trail: Traverse Rugged Cliffs and Remote Beaches

For a trek that immerses you in the rugged coastal beauty of Lake Superior, the Superior Coastal Trail is an adventurer's dream. Navigate challenging cliffs, traverse remote beaches, and witness the untamed power of the great lake. This trek offers not only physical challenges but also a deep connection with nature as you explore some of Thunder Bay's most secluded and pristine landscapes.

Pigeon River Headwaters Trail: Wilderness Trekking at Its Finest

Venture deep into Thunder Bay's wilderness with the Pigeon River Headwaters Trail. This trekking experience takes you through dense forests, across meandering rivers, and into the heart of the region's untouched beauty. As you trek, the only sounds are the rustling leaves, the songs of birds, and the whisper of the wind through the trees. This trail offers a true escape into the untamed north, where the raw beauty of Thunder Bay reveals itself in its purest form.

Eagle Canyon Suspension Bridge: A Unique Trekking Experience

For a thrilling and unique trekking adventure, head to the Eagle Canyon Suspension Bridge. This trail takes you through dense forests and across rugged terrain to reach the longest suspension bridge in Canada. As you traverse the swaying bridge suspended high above the canyon, you'll be rewarded with breathtaking views of the surrounding wilderness. This trek combines the excitement of suspension bridge crossings with the tranquility of Thunder Bay's pristine landscapes.

Black Bay Peninsula Trail: Remote Exploration and Wildlife Encounters

Embark on a remote trekking experience with the Black Bay Peninsula Trail. This trail leads you through the secluded Black Bay Peninsula, offering a chance to immerse yourself in the untouched wilderness. As you trek, keep an eye out for local wildlife, from majestic eagles soaring overhead to curious woodland creatures. The trail provides an intimate connection with nature, allowing you to experience Thunder Bay's wildlife and landscapes in their most authentic state.

Ouimet Canyon Loop Trail: Geological Wonders and Spectacular Views

For a trek that combines geological marvels with stunning panoramic views, the Ouimet Canyon Loop Trail is a must-visit. This trail takes you to the edge of Ouimet Canyon, where you can marvel at the dramatic cliffs and expansive vistas. The loop offers a variety of terrains, from forested paths to open viewpoints, providing a well-rounded trekking experience. Capture the essence of Thunder Bay's geological wonders as you traverse this captivating trail.

Casque Isles Trail: Coastal Beauty and Tranquil Shorelines

If you're seeking a longer trek with diverse landscapes, the Casque Isles Trail offers an extended adventure. Stretching along the Lake Superior coastline, this trail introduces you to picturesque

Thunder Bay Travel Guide 2024

shorelines, dense forests, and captivating viewpoints. The trek unfolds like a journey through different ecosystems, making it an ideal choice for those who wish to explore Thunder Bay's natural diversity over an extended period.

Tips for an Enjoyable Trekking Experience

- Check Trail Conditions: Before setting out, ensure that the trail you've chosen is open and safe. Thunder Bay's weather can vary, affecting trail conditions.
- Pack Essentials: Bring essentials like water, snacks, a map, and a compass. Wear sturdy, comfortable footwear suitable for the terrain.
- Respect Nature: Stay on designated trails to minimize impact, and respect wildlife by observing from a distance. Leave no trace to preserve Thunder Bay's pristine landscapes.
- Weather Preparedness: Thunder Bay's weather can be unpredictable. Dress in layers and be prepared for changing conditions, especially in higher elevations.
- Trail Etiquette: Be courteous to fellow trekkers. Yield to others on the trail, and follow any posted guidelines or rules.

The hiking and trekking trails of Thunder Bay are not just paths through nature; they are gateways to discovery, challenging you to explore the rugged beauty and untamed landscapes that define this remarkable region. Lace up your boots, embrace the spirit of adventure, and let Thunder Bay's trails guide you on an unforgettable journey.

Kayaking & Paddleboarding on Lake Superior

Coastal Exploration: Kayak Along Thunder Bay's Scenic Coastline

Set out on a kayaking adventure along Thunder Bay's scenic coastline, where the rugged beauty of the north meets the expansive waters of Lake Superior. Launch your kayak and paddle along the shore, exploring hidden coves and inlets. Marvel at the dramatic cliffs and rock formations that frame the shoreline, creating a picturesque backdrop for your aquatic journey. Coastal kayaking in Thunder Bay is not just a water excursion; it's a visual feast of nature's grandeur.

Sea Stack Encounters: Discovering Geological Marvels

Navigate your kayak to areas where Thunder Bay's geological wonders come to life. Encounter sea stacks—towering rock formations rising from the lake's depths. Paddle around these natural sculptures, appreciating the forces of nature that have shaped them over time. Your kayak becomes a gateway to uncovering the stories etched in stone, adding a geological dimension to your exploration.

Paddleboarding Serenity: Tranquil Moments on Lake Superior

For a serene and immersive experience, choose paddleboarding on the calm waters of Lake Superior. Glide across the lake's surface, feeling the gentle rhythm of the water beneath your board. Paddleboarding provides a unique vantage point, allowing you to soak in the tranquility of Thunder Bay's vast expanse. Whether you're a seasoned paddleboarder or a first-time enthusiast, Lake Superior's placid waters invite you to embrace moments of peaceful contemplation.

Sunset Paddle: A Magical Evening on the Water

As the day transitions into the evening, embark on a sunset paddle on Lake Superior. Launch your kayak or paddleboard as the sun dips below the horizon, casting a warm glow across the water. The evening sky transforms into a canvas of hues, reflecting on the lake's surface. Paddle in the quietude of twilight, basking in the magical ambiance that defines Thunder Bay's sunset paddling experience.

Isle Royale Exploration: Kayak to a Wilderness Archipelago

For the adventurous at heart, consider a kayaking expedition to Isle Royale, an archipelago in Lake Superior. Launch your kayak from Thunder Bay's shores, crossing the open waters to reach this remote wilderness destination. Explore pristine islands, camp along secluded shores, and witness the untamed beauty of Isle Royale—a journey that transforms your kayaking adventure into a multi-day exploration of nature untouched.

Safety Tips for Kayaking & Paddleboarding

- Wear Appropriate Gear: Equip yourself with a life jacket and suitable attire for water activities.
- Check Weather Conditions: Before heading out, check weather forecasts and be mindful of wind and wave conditions.
- Stay Hydrated: Bring sufficient water to stay hydrated during your paddling adventure.

Thunder Bay Travel Guide 2024

- Inform Others: Let someone know your paddling plans, including your expected return time.
- Respect Wildlife: Observe wildlife from a distance and avoid disturbing their natural behavior.

Kayaking and paddleboarding on Lake Superior offer an immersive encounter with the untamed north. As you paddle along the coastline, explore geological marvels, and embrace the tranquility of the lake, Thunder Bay's waters become more than a destination—they become a canvas for your outdoor adventure. Grab your paddle, embark on the journey, and let the serenity of Lake Superior guide you through the heart of Thunder Bay's aquatic wonders.

Cycling Routes & Scenic Bike Paths

Thunder Bay invites you to discover its untamed beauty from the saddle of your bike. With cycling routes that traverse diverse landscapes and scenic bike paths offering panoramic views, the adventure unfolds as you pedal through the heart of this northern gem.

Waterfront Trail: Coastal Beauty Unveiled by Bike

Start your cycling adventure with the Waterfront Trail, a picturesque route that follows the contours of Lake Superior's shoreline. Begin in the heart of Thunder Bay and pedal along the waterfront, where the rhythmic lapping of the lake accompanies your journey. Take in the breathtaking views of the expansive waters, distant horizons, and the rugged coastline. This scenic ride is a perfect introduction to the untamed north, offering a blend of urban charm and natural grandeur.

Trowbridge Falls Park to Centennial Park: Urban to Wilderness Ride

The transition from urban landscapes to wilderness wonders on the trail from Trowbridge Falls Park to Centennial Park. Begin amidst the lush greenery of Trowbridge Falls, where the cascading water adds a soothing soundtrack to your ride. Follow the path as it winds through forests and alongside the river, eventually leading you to Centennial Park. This cycling route provides a seamless blend of urban and natural beauty, showcasing Thunder Bay's diverse environments.

Kaministiquia River Heritage Trail: Historical Ride Along the River

Explore Thunder Bay's history while cycling along the Kaministiquia River Heritage Trail. This route takes you on a journey through time, passing by historical landmarks and sites that reflect the region's rich heritage. As you pedal alongside the river, discover the stories of Thunder Bay's past, from the fur trade era to the industrial developments that shaped this northern community.

Mount McKay Scenic Drive: Panoramic Views from Your Bike Seat

For a cycling experience that elevates your perspective, take on the Mount McKay Scenic Drive. This route, suitable for mountain bikes, leads you to the summit of Mount McKay, offering panoramic views of Thunder Bay and its surrounding wilderness. Challenge yourself with the ascent, and be rewarded with sweeping vistas that capture the untamed beauty of the north.

Sleeping Giant Parkway: Cycling Beneath the Sleeping Giant

Embark on a cycling journey beneath the watchful gaze of the Sleeping Giant along the Sleeping Giant Parkway. This route allows you to pedal through the beauty of Sleeping Giant Provincial Park, offering glimpses of the iconic formation from various angles. Traverse forests, cross bridges over tranquil streams and experience the unique charm of cycling within the embrace of Thunder Bay's natural wonders.

Boulevard Lake Circuit: Leisurely Ride Around an Urban Oasis

For a leisurely cycling experience around an urban oasis, choose the Boulevard Lake Circuit. This route encircles Boulevard Lake, providing a serene and accessible cycling path. Pedal at your own pace, enjoying the reflections of the surrounding trees on the lake's surface. The Boulevard Lake Circuit is ideal for those seeking a relaxed ride amidst Thunder Bay's urban greenery.

Tips for An Enjoyable Cycling Experience

- Check Your Bike: Ensure your bicycle is in good condition before setting out, with properly inflated tires and functioning brakes.
- Safety Gear: Wear a helmet and other appropriate safety gear to ensure a secure ride.
- Carry Essentials: Pack water, snacks, and any necessary tools for minor repairs during your ride.
- Follow Trail Rules: Adhere to trail rules and etiquette, including yielding to pedestrians and fellow cyclists.

- Weather Awareness: Check the weather forecast before your ride and dress accordingly. Thunder Bay's weather can be variable.

Cycling routes and scenic bike paths in Thunder Bay aren't just trails; they're gateways to immersive exploration. As you pedal along the waterfront, traverse historical routes, and embrace panoramic views, your bike becomes a conduit to Thunder Bay's untamed north. So, mount your bike, feel the wind on your face, and let the cycling routes guide you through the diverse landscapes of this northern haven.

Fishing & Hunting for Outdoor Enthusiasts

Superior Fishing Adventures: Cast Your Line into Lake Superior

Lake Superior, the world's largest freshwater lake, beckons fishing enthusiasts with its abundance of species. Set out on a fishing adventure and cast your line into the crystal-clear waters to reel in a variety of prized catches. From lake trout and salmon to walleye and whitefish, Lake Superior's diverse ecosystem promises a rewarding experience for anglers of all skill levels. Charter services are available for those looking to explore deeper waters and discover the best fishing spots.

Inland Lake Retreats: Tranquil Fishing Escapes

Beyond the vastness of Lake Superior, Thunder Bay offers numerous inland lakes that provide serene fishing escapes. Venture to secluded spots surrounded by forests and rolling hills, where the stillness of the water is broken only by the occasional splash of a catch. These inland retreats offer an opportunity for a peaceful day of fishing, allowing you to connect with nature in its purest form.

Hunting Expeditions: Navigate Thunder Bay's Wilderness

For those with a passion for the pursuit of game, Thunder Bay's wilderness becomes a sprawling hunting ground. From dense forests to open expanses, the region offers diverse habitats for various game species. Engage in responsible and sustainable hunting practices, respecting the natural balance of the ecosystem. Moose, deer, and small game are among the targets that draw hunting enthusiasts seeking an authentic and challenging experience in the untamed north.

Waterfowl Hunting: Wetland Adventures in Thunder Bay

Explore the wetlands and marshes of Thunder Bay through waterfowl hunting expeditions. The region's abundant water sources attract various waterfowl species, creating an ideal environment for hunters. Navigate through water channels, set up blinds along the shores, and experience the thrill of waterfowl hunting amidst the untamed beauty of Thunder Bay's wetlands.

Ice Fishing: Winter Pursuits on Frozen Lakes

As winter blankets Thunder Bay with snow and ice, the outdoor adventures continue with ice fishing. Lakes that were once liquid transform into frozen expanses, providing a unique opportunity for ice fishing enthusiasts. Bundle up against the winter chill, drill through the ice, and drop your line into the depths below. Ice fishing in Thunder Bay offers a serene and contemplative experience, combining the excitement of the catch with the tranquility of the winter landscape.

Thunder Bay Travel Guide 2024

Safety and Responsibility in Outdoor Pursuits

- Know the Regulations: Familiarize yourself with fishing and hunting regulations in Thunder Bay to ensure a legal and responsible outdoor experience.
- Wear Proper Gear: Equip yourself with appropriate clothing and gear for the specific outdoor activity and weather conditions.
- Respect Wildlife: Practice ethical and responsible behavior, respecting the natural habitats and wildlife encountered during your pursuits.
- Be Aware of Surroundings: Whether fishing or hunting, be mindful of your surroundings and adhere to safety protocols to ensure a secure outdoor experience.

Fishing and hunting in Thunder Bay extend beyond the mere pursuit of game; they offer an opportunity to immerse yourself in the untamed north's vast and diverse landscapes. From the depths of Lake Superior to the expanses of Thunder Bay's wilderness, each cast and each shot becomes a moment of connection with nature. So, gear up, embrace the thrill of the hunt, and let Thunder Bay's outdoor pursuits unfold before you in all their untamed glory.

Winter Wonderland: Skiing, Snowshoeing & Dog Sledding

As winter blankets Thunder Bay in a pristine layer of snow, the untamed north transforms into a winter wonderland, inviting outdoor enthusiasts to explore its frozen beauty. Skiing down snowy slopes, traversing quiet trails on snowshoes, and embarking on exhilarating dog sledding adventures are the gateways to discovering Thunder Bay's winter magic.

Skiing: Carve Through Snowy Slopes

Loch Lomond Ski Area: Downhill Thrills in the North

Loch Lomond Ski Area, nestled in the heart of Thunder Bay, offers downhill enthusiasts a playground of snowy slopes. Carve through powdery descents, navigate challenging trails, and soak in panoramic views of the surrounding winter landscape. From beginners to advanced skiers, Loch Lomond provides a range of slopes catering to different skill levels, making it an ideal destination for a day of downhill thrills.

Kamview Nordic Centre: Cross-Country Adventure

For those seeking the tranquility of cross-country skiing, Kamview Nordic Centre awaits. Explore meticulously groomed trails that wind through the serene winter forests of Thunder Bay. Cross-country skiing at Kamview Nordic Centre is not just a physical activity; it's a journey through snow-covered landscapes, where the only sounds are the swish of skis against snow and the whisper of the winter wind.

Snowshoeing: Traverse Tranquil Trails

Centennial Park Snowshoe Trails: Urban Winter Exploration

Centennial Park transforms into a winter oasis, offering snowshoers a network of trails to explore. Traverse the park's snow-covered terrain, meander through wooded areas, and enjoy the peaceful ambiance of a winter wonderland within the city limits. Centennial Park's snowshoe trails provide an accessible and serene escape for those looking to immerse themselves in the tranquility of a snowy landscape.

Sleeping Giant Provincial Park: Snowshoeing Amidst Giants

Venture into the iconic Sleeping Giant Provincial Park for a snowshoeing adventure amidst towering giants of snow-covered trees. The park's winter trails lead you through a majestic winter forest, offering a unique perspective on the giant's slumber. As you trek through the pristine snow, the stillness of the winter landscape becomes a canvas for your snowshoeing exploration.

Dog Sledding: A Thrilling Arctic Expedition

Embark on a thrilling dogsledding expedition with Chukuni Dogsled Tours, where a team of enthusiastic and well-trained dogs becomes your guide through the winter wilderness. Feel the rush of cold air on your face as you glide across frozen lakes and snow-covered trails. Dog sledding is not just a mode of transportation; it's an immersive experience that allows you to connect with the untamed north in its winter glory.

Ice Climbing: Conquer Frozen Cascades

For daring adventurers seeking an adrenaline rush, ice climbing at Orient Bay is an unparalleled experience. Frozen cascades along the shoreline of Lake Superior become vertical playgrounds for ice climbers. Strap on your crampons, wield your ice axes and ascend these icy heights for a thrilling winter challenge. Whether you're a seasoned climber or a first-timer, Orient Bay offers a variety of routes catering to different skill levels, ensuring an exhilarating adventure against the backdrop of the frozen lake.

Ice Skating: Glide Across Frozen Lakes

Boulevard Lake transforms into a natural ice rink during the winter months, providing a picturesque setting for ice skating enthusiasts. Lace-up your skates and glide across the frozen lake, surrounded by snow-covered trees and the serene winter landscape. Boulevard Lake's ice skating experience is a blend of outdoor recreation and tranquil moments, making it an ideal destination for those seeking a leisurely winter activity.

Winter Photography: Capture the Frozen Beauty

Winter in Thunder Bay offers a visual feast for photographers. Capture the frozen landscapes, snow-covered trees, and the ethereal beauty of the north in winter. Whether you're exploring the city's urban winter scenes or venturing into the wilderness, let your camera lens frame the magic of Thunder Bay's winter wonderland. From frosty details to expansive snowy vistas, winter photography becomes a means to preserve and share the enchanting moments of the untamed north in its frozen splendor.

Safety Tips for Winter Adventures:

- Dress in Layers: Layering provides insulation against the cold while allowing flexibility based on activity level.
- Stay Hydrated: Despite the cold, staying hydrated is crucial during winter activities.
- Know Your Limits: Be aware of your skill level and choose activities that match your experience.

- Check Equipment: Ensure that skiing, snowshoeing, and dog sledding equipment is in good condition before heading out.
- Winter Sun Protection: Use sunscreen and protective clothing to guard against the sun's reflective rays on snowy surfaces.

Thus, winter in Thunder Bay extends far beyond traditional activities; it's an invitation to explore a diverse palette of experiences. From the adrenaline-pumping thrill of ice climbing to the serene glide of ice skating, Thunder Bay's winter wonderland offers something for every winter enthusiast. Embrace the season's magic, layer up for warmth, and let the untamed north reveal its frozen beauty in every snowy adventure.

Chapter 8

Off-the-Beaten-Path Gems

Amethyst Mine

Nestled in the heart of Thunder Bay's wilderness, the Blue Point Amethyst Mine is a radiant jewel waiting to be unearthed. This off-the-beaten-path gem promises a unique and hands-on experience, allowing you to delve into the mesmerizing world of amethyst mining. As you embark on this excursion, prepare to be captivated by the allure of Thunder Bay's geological treasures.

Getting There

To reach the Blue Point Amethyst Mine, chart a course from Thunder Bay, immersing yourself in the scenic drive that unveils the pristine beauty of the surrounding landscape. As the road winds through forests and alongside lakeshores, the anticipation of discovering vibrant amethyst crystals builds with every mile.

Arrival and Overview

Upon arrival, the Blue Point Amethyst Mine welcomes you with open arms. Nestled amidst the rugged terrain, the mine provides an authentic setting for your amethyst exploration. Your journey begins with a warm greeting from knowledgeable guides who will equip you with the essential tools and insights needed to unearth your sparkling treasures.

Tools of the Trade

Before venturing into the mining grounds, familiarize yourself with the tools at your disposal. Equipped with a pickaxe, bucket, and gloves, you become an amateur geologist ready to extract amethyst specimens from the rich deposits beneath the surface. The thrill of discovering a piece of Thunder Bay's geological history is at your fingertips.

The Mining Experience

As you descend into the mine, the air becomes charged with excitement. The echo of picks against rock reverberates, creating a harmonious rhythm as you and your fellow adventurers unearth amethyst crystals. The vibrant hues of purple and violet emerge, glistening in the natural light, creating a kaleidoscopic display that showcases the geological wonders hidden beneath Thunder Bay's surface.

Digging for Your Treasures

Guided by your intuition and the guidance of experienced miners, you select your spot and begin to dig. The earth yields its treasures as your pickaxe strikes the amethyst-rich rock. Your bucket fills with raw amethyst clusters, each piece a testament to the geological forces that shaped Thunder Bay over millennia.

Sorting and Cleaning

Once your bucket is brimming with amethyst specimens, it's time to head to the sorting area. Here, under the guidance of experts, you sift through your findings, marveling at the unique shapes and sizes of each crystal. Engage in the meticulous process of cleaning your treasures, revealing the true brilliance and luster of Thunder Bay's amethyst.

The Mine Shop

After your mining adventure, a visit to the Mine Shop awaits. Here, you can browse a dazzling array of amethyst products, from polished crystals to exquisite jewelry crafted by local artisans.

Take a piece of Thunder Bay home with you, whether it's a small amethyst keepsake or a stunning statement piece that serves as a tangible reminder of your mining expedition.

Environmental Stewardship

As you revel in the beauty of your amethyst discoveries, remember the importance of responsible mining practices. The Blue Point Amethyst Mine is committed to environmental stewardship, ensuring that the natural surroundings are preserved for future generations. Your visit contributes to the sustainable exploration of Thunder Bay's geological treasures.

Tips for Your Amethyst Mining Adventure

Dress for the Occasion

Wear sturdy, closed-toe shoes and comfortable clothing suitable for outdoor exploration. A hat and sunscreen protect against the elements.

Stay Hydrated

Bring a water bottle to stay hydrated during your mining adventure. The fresh northern air and physical activity make it essential to keep yourself well-hydrated.

Listen to the Experts

The knowledgeable guides at the Blue Point Amethyst Mine are there to enhance your experience. Listen attentively to their insights and guidance for a fulfilling adventure.

Capture the Moment

Bring a camera or smartphone to capture the magic of your mining experience. Documenting your journey allows you to share the excitement with friends and family.

The Blue Point Amethyst Mine beckons you to embark on a journey of geological exploration in Thunder Bay's untamed north. As you dig, discover, and immerse yourself in the rich deposits of amethyst, you become part of the geological story written in the vibrant hues of Thunder Bay's crystals. This off-the-beaten-path adventure promises not just a collection of treasures but a deep connection with the geological wonders that define Thunder Bay's unique charm. Your amethyst mining adventure awaits – a radiant chapter in your exploration of the untamed north.

8.2 Kakabeka Falls

Embark on a journey to witness the awe-inspiring grandeur of Kakabeka Falls, a majestic natural wonder nestled in the heart of Thunder Bay's untamed north. Cascading with sheer magnificence, Kakabeka Falls invites you to experience the power and beauty of nature in a way that leaves an indelible mark on your travel memories.

Getting There

Your adventure begins with a scenic drive from Thunder Bay, weaving through lush landscapes and capturing glimpses of the surrounding wilderness. The anticipation builds as you approach Kakabeka Falls Provincial Park, where the rhythmic sound of rushing water signals your imminent encounter with one of nature's most spectacular creations.

Arrival and Overview

Upon arrival, the mist-laden air and the distant roar of falling water greet you, setting the stage for the spectacle that awaits. Kakabeka Falls stands as the second-highest waterfall in Ontario, a testament to the untamed forces that have shaped Thunder Bay's landscape over millennia.

The Gushing Majesty

As you approach the viewing platforms, Kakabeka Falls unfolds before you in all its gushing majesty. The Kaministiquia River plunges over the cliff's edge, creating a thunderous cascade that captivates the senses. Feel the cool mist on your face as you stand in the presence of this natural marvel, and let the sound of rushing water serenade you into a state of tranquil admiration.

Scenic Vantage Points

Explore the well-maintained trails and discover scenic vantage points that offer different perspectives of Kakabeka Falls. The park provides ample opportunities for photography, allowing you to capture the falls from various angles and document the sheer power and beauty that define this natural spectacle.

Hiking Trails

For those seeking a closer encounter, Kakabeka Falls Provincial Park offers hiking trails that wind through the surrounding wilderness. As you traverse these paths, the invigorating scent of pine and the sound of rustling leaves accompany you, creating a sensory journey that complements the visual splendor of the falls.

Seasonal Changes

Kakabeka Falls undergoes captivating transformations throughout the seasons. In the winter, witness the falls adorned in a glittering coat of ice, creating a magical winter wonderland. Spring brings a surge in water volume, enhancing the falls' power, while autumn dresses the surrounding foliage in a vibrant tapestry of colors, framing Kakabeka Falls in a breathtaking panorama.

Thunder Bay Travel Guide 2024

Interpretive Center

Enhance your Kakabeka Falls experience by visiting the Interpretive Center. Immerse yourself in the geological and cultural history of the falls through exhibits and displays. Gain insights into the Indigenous significance of Kakabeka Falls and its role in the region's rich tapestry of stories.

Picnicking and Relaxation

Extend your stay and savor the natural beauty by enjoying a picnic in the designated areas. The park provides a tranquil setting, inviting you to unwind amidst the sounds of nature. Whether you choose to sit by the falls or find a shaded spot along the riverbank, Kakabeka Falls offers a serene escape.

Tips for Your Kakabeka Falls Adventure

Pack Essentials

Bring essentials such as sunscreen, water, and comfortable walking shoes. The terrain around Kakabeka Falls is accessible but may involve walking.

Check Seasonal Events

Stay informed about seasonal events and festivals happening at Kakabeka Falls Provincial Park. These events often provide unique opportunities to engage with the local community and learn more about the falls.

Respect Nature

Admire Kakabeka Falls from designated viewing areas and respect park guidelines. Responsible tourism ensures the preservation of this natural marvel for future generations.

Kakabeka Falls beckons you to witness the unbridled beauty of Thunder Bay's natural landscape. As you stand in the presence of this cascading masterpiece, you become a part of the ongoing story written by the powerful forces that have shaped Kakabeka Falls over time. Your adventure to Kakabeka Falls is not just a journey to witness nature's grandeur but an opportunity to connect with the untamed north in a profound and memorable way. The falls await – a breathtaking chapter in your exploration of Thunder Bay's natural marvels.

Sleeping Giant Provincial Park

Prepare to be immersed in the untamed beauty of Thunder Bay as you venture into the wilderness expanse of Sleeping Giant Provincial Park. This natural sanctuary, named after the iconic Sleeping Giant formation, invites you on an exploration that transcends the ordinary. As you step into this vast provincial park, you are embarking on a journey that promises panoramic vistas, diverse ecosystems, and an adventure that unfolds beneath the watchful gaze of the Sleeping Giant.

Getting There

Your odyssey begins with a drive from Thunder Bay, winding through picturesque landscapes that gradually reveal the natural wonders awaiting you. The anticipation builds as you approach Sleeping Giant Provincial Park, where the allure of unspoiled wilderness and the promise of outdoor adventure beckon.

Arrival and Overview

Upon entering the park, a sense of tranquility envelops you. The park's expansive territory offers a diverse range of landscapes, from dense forests to rocky cliffs and pristine lakeshores. Prepare to be captivated by the harmonious blend of natural elements that define Sleeping Giant Provincial Park.

The Sleeping Giant Formation

The centerpiece of the park, the Sleeping Giant, commands your attention. Gaze upon the colossal rock formation that resembles a reclining giant, a geological marvel shaped by ancient forces. Your journey through the park unfolds against the backdrop of this iconic symbol, adding a touch of mystique to your wilderness adventure.

Hiking Trails

Sleeping Giant Provincial Park boasts a network of hiking trails that cater to all levels of adventurers. Choose a trail that aligns with your preference, whether it's a stroll through wooded pathways or a challenging ascent to panoramic lookouts. Each trail promises a unique perspective of the park's natural beauty.

Sea Lion Rock Trail

Embark on the Sea Lion Rock Trail, a moderate hike that rewards you with stunning views of Lake Superior and the surrounding landscape. As you navigate through lush forests and rocky terrain, the rhythmic sound of waves accompanies your journey to the Sea Lion Rock lookout, offering a prime vantage point for capturing the untamed beauty of the park.

Top of the Giant Trail

For a more adventurous spirit, conquer the Top of the Giant Trail. This challenging ascent takes you to the summit of the Sleeping Giant, where a breathtaking panorama unfolds. Survey the vastness of Lake Superior and revel in the sense of accomplishment that comes with reaching the pinnacle of this geological giant.

Wildlife Encounters

Keep a keen eye out for the park's diverse wildlife. From woodland creatures like red foxes and white-tailed deer to the possibility of spotting bald eagles soaring overhead, Sleeping Giant Provincial Park provides opportunities for wildlife enthusiasts to connect with the natural inhabitants of this pristine wilderness.

Kayaking and Canoeing

Navigate the crystal-clear waters of Marie Louise Lake or other inland lakes within the park by embarking on a kayaking or canoeing adventure. The peaceful waters surrounded by lush greenery offer a serene escape, allowing you to paddle at your own pace and absorb the tranquility of the park.

Camping Amidst Nature's Symphony

Extend your wilderness experience by camping within the park. Choose from various campgrounds that immerse you in nature's symphony – the rustling leaves, the gentle lapping of water, and the distant calls of wildlife. Camping at Sleeping Giant Provincial Park is an opportunity to truly disconnect and embrace the serenity of the untamed north.

Tips for Your Sleeping Giant Provincial Park Adventure

Check Trail Conditions

Before embarking on a hike, check trail conditions at the park's visitor center. This ensures a safe and enjoyable exploration of Sleeping Giant Provincial Park.

Pack Essentials

Ensure you have necessities like water, insect repellent, and suitable footwear with you. The park's varied terrain may require different preparations depending on your chosen activities.

Respect the Wilderness

Adhere to Leave No Trace principles. Respect the park's flora and fauna by minimizing your impact on the environment, leaving it as pristine as you found it.

Sleeping Giant Provincial Park beckons you to step into the heart of Thunder Bay's wilderness. As you explore the diverse landscapes, conquer challenging trails, and immerse yourself in the tranquility of the park, you become a participant in the unfolding story of Sleeping Giant. Your wilderness odyssey at Sleeping Giant Provincial Park is not just an adventure; it's a journey of discovery, where nature's wonders and the untamed north intertwine to create an unforgettable chapter in your exploration of Thunder Bay's natural treasures. The park awaits – a vast canvas for your wilderness escapade.

Terry Fox Monument

Your journey through Thunder Bay's untamed north takes on a poignant and inspirational note as you encounter the Terry Fox Monument. This monument, dedicated to a true Canadian hero, invites you to connect with the spirit of perseverance and determination that defined Terry Fox's remarkable journey. As you stand before this tribute, you become part of a legacy that transcends physical boundaries and embodies the indomitable human spirit.

Getting There

From Thunder Bay, embark on a reflective drive to reach the Terry Fox Monument. As you approach, the monument's silhouette against the northern sky signals that you are about to witness a testament to courage and resilience.

Arrival and Overview

Upon arrival, the Terry Fox Monument stands as a beacon of inspiration. Set against the backdrop of Lake Superior, this powerful tribute honors Terry Fox's Marathon of Hope – a journey that captured the hearts of Canadians and people around the world. The monument reflects the enduring impact of Terry Fox's mission to raise awareness for cancer research.

Terry Fox's Marathon of Hope

Immerse yourself in the story of Terry Fox's Marathon of Hope, a cross-country run undertaken by Terry in 1980 to raise funds for cancer research. Learn about his unwavering determination and the challenges he faced as he ran a marathon each day, covering a staggering distance before his journey was cut short. The monument captures the essence of Terry Fox's selfless quest and his enduring legacy.

Monument Design and Symbolism

As you explore the monument, take note of its design and the symbolism woven into every element. The bronze statue of Terry Fox in mid-stride encapsulates his determined spirit. The artificial leg, a testament to his battle with cancer, becomes a symbol of hope and resilience. The open road before him represents the uncharted path he embarked upon, inspiring others to follow in his footsteps.

Reflective Surroundings

The monument's surroundings offer a reflective space to contemplate Terry Fox's legacy. Overlooking Lake Superior, the location provides a tranquil atmosphere that encourages introspection. The vastness of the northern landscape mirrors the boundless possibilities that emerge when one person's vision ignites a movement.

Participate in the Annual Terry Fox Run

If your visit coincides with the annual Terry Fox Run, consider participating in this community event that continues Terry's mission. Join fellow participants in a run, walk, or wheelchair ride to raise funds for cancer research. The run serves as a living tribute to Terry Fox's enduring impact and the collective effort to carry his legacy forward.

Leaving Your Mark

Become a part of the ongoing legacy by leaving a personal message or token at the monument. Many visitors express their admiration for Terry Fox's courage and resilience by leaving tokens of appreciation, creating a communal space that reflects the collective gratitude and inspiration drawn from his remarkable journey.

Tips for Your Visit

Bring Tokens of Tribute

Consider bringing a small token, such as a ribbon or a written note, to leave at the monument as a gesture of tribute and appreciation.

Check for Events

Stay informed about any events or activities happening at the Terry Fox Monument, especially if you plan to participate in the annual Terry Fox Run.

Take Time for Reflection

The reflective atmosphere around the monument invites you to take a moment of contemplation. Allow yourself the space to absorb the significance of Terry Fox's journey and the impact it has had on cancer research.

The Terry Fox Monument stands as more than a physical structure; it is a living tribute to a hero whose legacy resonates far beyond Thunder Bay. As you stand before this monument, you are not just a visitor; you become part of a collective narrative of hope, perseverance, and the enduring power of the human spirit. The Terry Fox Monument invites you to reflect, honor, and carry forward the torch of determination that continues to inspire generations. Your visit is not just a pause in your journey; it's a moment to connect with a profound legacy that echoes through the northern landscape. The monument awaits – a testament to courage, hope, and the limitless potential of the human heart.

Hidden Local Haunts & Unexpected Delights

Venture beyond the well-trodden paths and discover the heartbeat of Thunder Bay in its hidden local haunts and unexpected delights. I invite you to explore the lesser-known treasures that add a layer of authenticity to your Thunder Bay experience. From tucked-away eateries to secret scenic spots, these hidden gems promise to unveil the city's character in ways that may surprise and delight.

Cozy Cafés and Local Hangouts

Dive into the local scene by seeking out hidden cafés and hangouts favored by Thunder Bay residents. Whether it's a quaint coffee shop tucked down a side street or a hidden gem with a cozy ambiance, these spots offer more than just a cup of coffee.

Artisanal Boutiques and Nooks

Wander through the city's neighborhoods and explore artisanal boutiques and tucked-away nooks. These hidden spots often house unique finds crafted by local artisans. From handmade jewelry to bespoke home décor, discover one-of-a-kind pieces that tell a story of Thunder Bay's creative spirit.

Street Art and Murals

Thunder Bay's streets are adorned with vibrant street art and murals, waiting to be discovered in hidden corners and alleys. Take a stroll through the city, keeping an eye out for these unexpected bursts of creativity. Each mural contributes to Thunder Bay's urban tapestry, showcasing the diversity of artistic expression.

Parks and Green Spaces Off the Beaten Path

Escape the well-known parks and explore green spaces off the beaten path. These hidden parks may offer serene lakeside views, secluded picnic spots, or quiet trails that lead to unexpected vistas. Embrace the tranquility and natural beauty that Thunder Bay's lesser-known green spaces have to offer.

Culinary Secrets

Indulge in Thunder Bay's culinary scene by seeking out hidden gems that cater to local flavors and international delights. Unassuming eateries with delectable dishes, food trucks tucked into surprising corners, and family-run establishments often hold the keys to culinary experiences that go beyond the expected.

Local Events and Pop-Up Experiences

Stay tuned to local event calendars for pop-up experiences and hidden events that may not be widely advertised. These impromptu gatherings, whether it's a local market, live performance, or community event, provide an opportunity to connect with Thunder Bay's dynamic and vibrant community spirit.

Historical Hideaways

Delve into Thunder Bay's history by exploring historical hideaways and lesser-known landmarks. These sites may not be featured in mainstream tourist guides, but they hold stories of the city's past, offering a more nuanced understanding of its rich heritage.

Tips for Uncovering Hidden Gems

Chat with Locals

Strike up conversations with locals and ask for recommendations. Residents often hold the keys to Thunder Bay's best-kept secrets.

Explore Neighborhoods

Venture into different neighborhoods and meander through local streets. Hidden gems are often nestled within the fabric of residential areas.

Follow Social Media and Blogs

Stay connected with Thunder Bay's local scene by following social media accounts and blogs that highlight hidden gems and unexpected delights.

As you embark on the quest to uncover Thunder Bay's hidden local haunts and unexpected delights, remember that the true essence of the city lies beyond the well-known attractions. These hidden gems are the threads that weave a more intricate and authentic narrative of Thunder Bay's character. Embrace the sense of curiosity, wander through hidden alleyways, and allow yourself to be surprised by the unexpected treasures that await in the heart of Thunder Bay. Your exploration of these hidden local haunts is not just a journey off the beaten path; it's an invitation to connect with the pulse of the city and discover its soul in the places less traveled. Thunder Bay's hidden gems await – a testament to the city's capacity to surprise and delight.

Part 4

Essential Information & Resources

Chapter 9

Practicalities and Resources

Embarking on your Thunder Bay adventure requires careful consideration of practicalities and access to essential resources. Here, I'll navigate the crucial aspects of visas, currency exchange, and other practicalities to ensure your journey to Canada's untamed north is seamless.

Visas & Currency Exchange

Your journey to Thunder Bay begins with understanding the entry requirements based on your nationality. Here's a tailored guide for travelers from the United States, Europe, Australia, and Japan:

For U.S. Travelers

As a U.S. citizen, you are in luck. For short visits (up to 180 days), no visa is required. You'll only need a valid passport. Make sure that your passport remains valid for at least six months beyond your planned departure date. Thunder Bay warmly welcomes you without the need for additional paperwork.

For European Travelers

If you're traveling from a European Union (EU) country, you can enjoy visa-exempt entry for up to 90 days within a 180-day period. A valid passport is your key to Thunder Bay. However, for non-EU European countries, check the specific visa requirements to ensure a smooth entry.

For Australian Travelers

Australian citizens, like their U.S. counterparts, do not require a visa for visits up to 180 days. A valid passport is sufficient, but remember to check the expiration date. Thunder Bay awaits your exploration without the hassle of visa applications.

For Japanese Travelers

Japan benefits from a visa-exempt status for short stays (up to 90 days). A valid passport is your gateway to Thunder Bay. Ensure your travel document remains valid throughout your stay for a seamless adventure.

Currency Exchange

Navigating currency exchange is vital to ensure smooth transactions during your Thunder Bay journey. Here's a detailed guide on managing currencies:

U.S. Dollars (USD)

While Thunder Bay operates in Canadian Dollars (CAD), U.S. dollars are widely accepted in many establishments. However, it's advisable to exchange some currency for convenience, especially in more remote areas. Currency exchange services are available at Thunder Bay International Airport and various banks in the city.

Euro (EUR), Australian Dollar (AUD), Japanese Yen (JPY), and Other Currencies

For travelers from Europe, Australia, Japan, and other regions, exchanging your currency for Canadian Dollars is recommended. Thunder Bay's banking institutions, currency exchange offices, and ATMs provide accessible options. Be aware of potential fees, and consider exchanging a portion of your currency in advance for initial expenses.

Tips for Currency Management

- ATM Accessibility: Thunder Bay boasts a network of ATMs, ensuring convenient access to Canadian Dollars. Inquire with your bank about fees associated with international withdrawals.
- Credit Card Usage: Major credit cards are widely accepted in Thunder Bay. Notify your bank of your travel dates to avoid any interruptions in the use of your card.
- Currency Exchange Rates: Stay informed about exchange rates before your journey. Online tools and currency converter apps can assist in real-time rate checks.
- Emergency Cash: Keep a small amount of Canadian currency for emergencies or situations where card payments may not be accepted.

Health & Safety Tips

Your well-being is paramount as you embark on your adventure to Thunder Bay. Understanding health and safety tips ensures a worry-free exploration of the untamed north.

Health Preparations

Travel Insurance: Begin your journey by considering comprehensive travel insurance. This essential safeguard covers medical emergencies, trip cancellations, and unexpected events. Confirm that your insurance extends to outdoor activities if you plan to engage in adventurous pursuits.

Healthcare Services: Thunder Bay offers quality healthcare services to ensure your well-being during your stay. Familiarize yourself with the location of hospitals, clinics, and pharmacies. The Thunder Bay Regional Health Sciences Centre stands as a major healthcare facility, providing peace of mind for any unforeseen medical needs.

Vaccinations: Stay proactive about your health by checking with your healthcare provider for recommended vaccinations. Ensure that routine vaccinations are up to date, and inquire about specific travel vaccines that might be necessary for your journey.

Safety Guidelines

Wildlife Awareness: As you immerse yourself in Thunder Bay's wilderness, be mindful of the diverse wildlife that calls the region home. Familiarize yourself with safety measures, especially if engaging in outdoor activities. Consider carrying bear spray if venturing into more remote areas to ensure your safety and the wildlife's well-being.

Weather Preparedness: Thunder Bay experiences diverse weather conditions, with cold winters and warm summers. Dressing appropriately is key to your comfort and safety. Stay informed about weather forecasts, especially if you plan to engage in winter activities. Layers are your friend, allowing you to adapt to changing conditions.

Emergency Contacts: Prioritize your safety by saving important numbers in your phone.

If you encounter an emergency, please dial 911 for prompt assistance. Additionally, note the contact information for the nearest embassy or consulate, as well as your country's embassy or consulate in Canada. Having this information readily available ensures prompt assistance in various situations.

Additional Tips for Health and Safety

- Local Safety Guidelines: Familiarize yourself with any specific safety guidelines provided by local authorities. This may include information on hiking trails, water safety, and other outdoor activities.
- Hydration and Nutrition: Maintain your well-being by staying hydrated and nourished. Carry a reusable water bottle to ensure you have access to water during your explorations. Explore local cuisine but be mindful of any dietary restrictions or preferences.
- Personal Safety Measures: Practice general safety measures such as being aware of your surroundings, securing your belongings, and following any posted guidelines at tourist attractions and natural sites.
- First Aid Kit: Pack a basic first aid kit with essentials like bandages, pain relievers, any necessary prescription medications, and personal items tailored to your health needs.

By prioritizing your health and adhering to safety guidelines, you set the foundation for a rewarding and secure adventure in Thunder Bay. Whether you're exploring the outdoors, enjoying cultural experiences, or indulging in local cuisine, these tips ensure that your well-being remains at the forefront of your journey.

Transportation Options & Local Transit

Thunder Bay's expansive landscapes and unique attractions call for strategic transportation planning. Explore the transportation options available to make the most of your adventure in Canada's untamed north.

Getting to Thunder Bay

Air Travel: Thunder Bay International Airport (YQT) serves as a gateway to this northern gem. Direct flights connect Thunder Bay to major Canadian cities and international hubs. Airlines like Air Canada and WestJet offer convenient options for reaching Thunder Bay. Ensure you book your flights well in advance to secure the best rates.

Road Travel: If you prefer the scenic route, consider a road trip to Thunder Bay. The Trans-Canada Highway provides breathtaking views as you make your way to this northern city. Plan your journey, taking into account the distance and potential stops along the way to make the most of your road travel experience.

Local Transit in Thunder Bay

Public Transit: Thunder Bay Transit offers comprehensive bus services throughout the city, providing an efficient way to navigate urban areas. Familiarize yourself with the routes and schedules to plan your city exploration seamlessly. Bus passes are available for purchase, offering flexibility for multiple rides.

Car Rentals: To fully embrace the freedom of exploring Thunder Bay and its surrounding areas, consider renting a car. Various car rental agencies, including well-known brands like Enterprise and Budget, operate at Thunder Bay International Airport and within the city. Having your vehicle allows you to set your own pace and venture off the beaten path.

Taxi Services: Taxis are readily available in Thunder Bay, offering a convenient option for point-to-point transportation. Note the contact numbers for reliable taxi services, and consider using ride-sharing apps for additional convenience, ensuring you have options for getting around the city.

Navigating Transportation Tips

- Public Transit Efficiency: Thunder Bay Transit operates efficiently, making it a viable option for city travel. Check the schedules and routes in advance, and consider purchasing a transit pass if you plan to use public transportation frequently.
- Car Rentals for Exploration: Renting a car provides the flexibility to explore Thunder Bay and its scenic surroundings. Make sure you possess a valid driver's license, and acquaint yourself with the traffic regulations in the local area. Plan your itinerary to include both city attractions and the natural wonders beyond.
- Airport Transportation: If you're arriving by air, plan your transportation from Thunder Bay International Airport to your accommodation. Many hotels offer shuttle services, or you can opt for taxis or rental cars available at the airport.
- Weather Considerations: Be mindful of weather conditions, especially if you plan to explore Thunder Bay's outdoor attractions. Winter weather, in particular, can affect road conditions, so stay informed and plan accordingly.

Additional Tips for Smooth Travel

- Plan Ahead: Research your transportation options and plan your routes in advance. This ensures a smoother and more enjoyable travel experience, allowing you to make the most of your time in Thunder Bay.
- Local Insights: Don't hesitate to ask locals for transportation tips or recommendations. They may provide valuable insights

into the best routes, hidden gems, and local transportation nuances.

- Digital Navigation Tools: Leverage digital navigation tools such as GPS apps or maps on your smartphone to navigate the city and surrounding areas confidently.

By considering your transportation options and planning accordingly, you set the stage for a seamless exploration of Thunder Bay's unique blend of urban charm and natural wonders. Whether you choose public transit, opt for a rental car, or embrace a mix of transportation modes, the untamed north awaits your discovery.

Communication & Emergency Services

Ensuring effective communication and being aware of emergency services are crucial aspects of your Thunder Bay adventure. Navigate the untamed north with confidence by understanding the communication essentials and having access to emergency services.

Communication Essentials

SIM Cards and Mobile Networks

Local SIM Cards: Upon your arrival in Thunder Bay, consider purchasing a local SIM card for your phone. This allows you to have a local number and access Canadian mobile networks seamlessly.

International Roaming: Alternatively, check with your mobile provider for international roaming options. Ensure that your phone is unlocked before your journey.

Internet Access

Wi-Fi Availability: Many accommodations, cafes, and public spaces in Thunder Bay provide Wi-Fi access. Confirm the availability of your accommodation and explore local cafes for reliable internet connections.

Portable Wi-Fi Devices: For constant connectivity, consider renting portable Wi-Fi devices, especially if you plan to venture into areas with limited network coverage.

Embassy or Consulate Contacts

Country's Representation: Note the contact information for your country's embassy or consulate in Canada. This information serves as a crucial resource for assistance in various situations, including lost passports or emergency evacuations.

Tips for Effective Communication

Stay Informed

Local News Sources: Stay updated on local news and events by tuning in to local news channels or reading regional newspapers. This helps you stay informed about any developments that may impact your stay.

Useful Phrases

Basic Phrases: While English is widely spoken in Thunder Bay, learning a few basic phrases in French may be helpful. Residents value the effort, and it has the potential to enrich your overall encounter.

Digital Communication

Social Media: Utilize social media platforms for real-time updates on local events, attractions, and weather conditions. Follow local pages and hashtags to stay connected with the Thunder Bay community.

Emergency Contacts

Save Important Numbers: Aside from 911, save other important numbers in your phone, including non-emergency police lines, local hospitals, and your country's embassy or consulate.

Navigating Communication Tips

Network Coverage

Check Coverage Maps: Before venturing into remote areas, check network coverage maps to ensure you have reliable connectivity. Certain regions may have limited mobile network access.

Communication Plans

Inform Your Contacts: Share your travel itinerary and accommodation details with trusted contacts. This provides an additional layer of safety, as someone will know your whereabouts.

Local Assistance

Visitor Information Centers: Thunder Bay has visitor information centers that can assist with local information and provide guidance on communication services. Visit these centers for maps, brochures, and additional support.

Cultural Sensitivity

Respect Local Customs: While communicating, be mindful of cultural nuances and practice respectful communication. Thunder Bay's community values inclusivity and appreciates visitors who embrace local customs.

By prioritizing effective communication and staying informed about emergency services, you enhance your Thunder Bay experience. Whether you're sharing your journey with loved ones or seeking assistance in unforeseen circumstances, these communication essentials ensure you navigate the untamed north with confidence and connectivity.

Final Thoughts and Recommendations

As you conclude the "Thunder Bay Travel Guide 2024," it's not just the end of a guidebook but the beginning of an extraordinary adventure. Thunder Bay, situated in Canada's untamed north, beckons you with its stunning natural beauty, diverse outdoor activities, and off-the-beaten-path wonders. Let's recap your journey and offer some final thoughts and recommendations for an unforgettable experience in this captivating destination.

Reflecting on Thunder Bay's Natural Splendor

Your exploration of Thunder Bay commences with its natural wonders – a tapestry of landscapes that unfolds with each turn of the page. Lake Superior, the world's largest freshwater lake, sets the stage for an awe-inspiring journey. The rugged beauty of Sleeping Giant Provincial Park, the thundering Kakabeka Falls, and the tranquil Blue Point Amethyst Mine are just glimpses into Thunder Bay's remarkable canvas of natural marvels.

As you venture into this untamed north, immerse yourself in the sheer beauty that surrounds you. Take the time to breathe in the fresh air, absorb the panoramic views, and revel in the serenity that only a place like Thunder Bay can offer. Whether you find yourself standing before the iconic Sleeping Giant or marveling at the hues of amethyst in the mine, each encounter with nature here is an invitation to connect with the wild.

Embarking on Outdoor Adventures

The guide has equipped you with the knowledge to embrace Thunder Bay's adventurous spirit. From the tranquility of scenic walks to the thrill of dog sledding in a winter wonderland, the untamed north unfolds as a playground for every outdoor enthusiast. Hiking trails lead you through diverse landscapes, kayaking excursions take you onto the expansive Lake Superior, and the call of the wilderness echoes in the heart of Thunder Bay.

Your journey isn't just about observing nature; it's about becoming a part of it. Engage in the activities that resonate with your spirit – cast a line into the crystal-clear waters, feel the rush of wind on a cycling route, or traverse snow-covered trails in the heart of winter. Thunder Bay invites you to be more than a spectator; it invites you to be a participant in the grand symphony of its natural wonders.

Unveiling Off-the-Beaten-Path Gems

Beyond the well-trodden paths lie the hidden gems of Thunder Bay, waiting to be discovered by the discerning traveler. The Blue Point Amethyst Mine, where you can unearth your sparkling treasures, is a testament to the geological wonders that lie beneath the surface. Kakabeka Falls captivates with its breathtaking descent, while Sleeping Giant Provincial Park reveals the untold stories of the land.

Tread the off-the-beaten paths with curiosity and an open heart. The Terry Fox Monument stands as a tribute to resilience and courage, urging you to reflect on the indomitable spirit of the human journey. Seek out the local haunts and unexpected delights

– Thunder Bay's untamed north rewards those who venture beyond the expected.

Tailoring Your Adventure with Itineraries

The guide's carefully crafted itineraries cater to diverse travel styles, ensuring that Thunder Bay becomes not just a destination but a personalized experience. Whether you're embarking on a family-friendly weekend, a solo explorer's journey, a romantic escapade, or an action-packed adventure, Thunder Bay unfolds its wonders in alignment with your preferences.

Consider the itineraries as a blueprint for your Thunder Bay adventure, a starting point to curate moments that resonate with your interests and desires. Each chapter within the guide offers a pathway to tailor your journey, allowing you to shape your experience in this untamed north.

Immersing in Thunder Bay's History and Culture

Thunder Bay isn't just a haven for nature enthusiasts; it's a canvas that tells the tales of a rich history and vibrant culture. Indigenous heritage weaves through the very fabric of the city, and the fur trade legacy comes to life at Fort William Historical Park. The arts and culture scene, from museums to festivals, invites you to immerse yourself in Thunder Bay's diverse tapestry.

Take the opportunity to delve into the past, learning from the stories etched in the city's architecture, art, and traditions. The fusion of flavors in Thunder Bay's culinary scene offers a taste of the region's cultural diversity. As you explore, let the history and culture of Thunder Bay become threads in the narrative of your adventure.

Practicalities, Resources, and Essential Information

In the final chapters, the guide addresses practicalities, resources, and essential information crucial for a seamless Thunder Bay experience. Understanding visa requirements, managing currency exchange, prioritizing health and safety, and navigating transportation options ensure that every aspect of your journey is well-prepared.

Utilize the resources provided, from maps and guidebooks to online platforms and mobile apps, to enhance your Thunder Bay exploration. Stay connected with the local culture, stay safe with health and safety tips, and seamlessly navigate the untamed north with information on transportation and emergency services.

A Tapestry of Memories: Your Thunder Bay Journey

As you close the pages of the "Thunder Bay Travel Guide 2024," envision not just the end of a guidebook but the beginning of your personal memories. Thunder Bay, with its stunning natural beauty, diverse outdoor activities, and hidden treasures, has invited you to partake in an adventure beyond the ordinary.

Each recommendation, tip, and insight offered in this guide is a thread in the narrative of your Thunder Bay journey. Whether you're gazing upon the vastness of Lake Superior, embarking on a solo exploration, or uncovering the history and culture that shapes Thunder Bay, the untamed north becomes more than a destination – it becomes a part of your story.

In the untamed north of Canada lies a city that transcends the ordinary – Thunder Bay. It is a destination where nature's grandeur meets human curiosity, where adventure is not just a possibility but a promise. This guide is your invitation to embark on a journey that goes beyond the expected, where every step reveals a new facet of this untamed wilderness. Your adventure awaits – let Thunder Bay captivate your senses and etch its place in your travel memories.

Acknowledgments

I would like to express my gratitude to the people of Thunder Bay for their warm hospitality, openness, and willingness to share their beautiful home with travelers from around the world. Your kindness has made this guide more than just a collection of information; it's a reflection of the heart and soul of Thunder Bay.

I want to acknowledge you, the traveler. Your curiosity, enthusiasm, and willingness to explore this incredible destination have made this journey worthwhile. I hope this guide has enriched your Thunder Bay experience and provided you with the tools to create lasting memories in this remarkable part of the world.

As you venture forth on future adventures, may you carry the spirit of Thunder Bay with you, and may your travels be filled with the same wonder, appreciation, and discovery that you've found here.

Thunder Bay Travel Planner 2024

Thunder Bay

Date:_____

Town:_____

Travel Planner 2024

Monday	Tuesday	Wednesday

Thursday	Friday	Saturday

Checklist	Note

Thunder Bay Travel Guide 2024

Thunder Bay

Date:_____

Town:_____

Travel Planner 2024

Monday	Tuesday	Wednesday

Thursday	Friday	Saturday

Checklist	Note

Thunder Bay

Date:_____

Town:_____

Travel Planner 2024

Monday	Tuesday	Wednesday

Thursday	Friday	Saturday

Checklist	Note

Thunder Bay

Travel Planner 2024

Monday	Tuesday	Wednesday

Thursday	Friday	Saturday

Checklist	Note

Thunder Bay

Travel Planner 2024

Monday	Tuesday	Wednesday

Thursday	Friday	Saturday

Checklist	Note

Thunder Bay

Date:_____

Town:_____

Travel Planner 2024

Monday	Tuesday	Wednesday

Thursday	Friday	Saturday

Checklist	Note

Thunder Bay Travel Itinerary 2024

Name:		Duration of Stay:

Hotel Name:		

Arrival Date:		Flight No:

Days	What To Do	Budget
01		
02		
03		
04		
Note		

Thunder Bay Travel Guide 2024

Name:		Duration of Stay:
Hotel Name:		Flight No:
Arrival Date:		

Days	What To Do	Budget
01		
02		
03		
04		
Note		

Thunder Bay Travel Guide 2024

Name:		Duration of Stay:

Hotel Name:

Flight No:

Arrival Date:

Days	What To Do	Budget
01		
02		
03		
04		
Note		

Thunder Bay Travel Guide 2024

Name:	Duration of Stay:
Hotel Name:	Flight No:
Arrival Date:	

Days	What To Do	Budget
01		
02		
03		
04		
Note		

161

Name:	Duration of Stay:
Hotel Name:	Flight No:
Arrival Date:	

Days	What To Do	Budget
01		
02		
03		
04		
Note		

162

Printed in Great Britain
by Amazon

38387444R00096